C000017616

SHAMBHALA POCKET LIBRARY

THE CLOUD
OF UNKNOWING

_____

TRANSLATION BY

Carmen Acevedo Butcher

SHAMBHALA · Boulder · 2018

SHAMBHALA PUBLICATIONS, INC.
4720 Walnut Street
Boulder, Colorado 80301
www.shambhala.com

This translation was originally published as *The Cloud of Unknowing with
the Book of Privy Counsel* (2009). This edition contains the complete
translation but omits *The Book of Privy Counsel*.

9 8 7 6 5 4 3 2 1

Printed in the United States of America

⊗ This edition is printed on acid-free paper that meets the
American National Standards Institute z39.48 Standard.
♲ This book is printed on 30% postconsumer recycled paper.
For more information please visit us at www.shambhala.com.
Distributed in the United States by Penguin Random House LLC
and in Canada by Random House of Canada Ltd

Designed by Lora Zorian

LIBRARY OF CONGRESS CATALOGING-IN-PUBLICATION DATA
Names: Butcher, Carmen Acevedo, translator.
Title: The cloud of unknowing/translated by Carmen Acevedo Butcher.
Other titles: Cloud of unknowing. | Book of privy counsel.
Description: Boulder: Shambhala, 2018. | This translation originally
published: 2009. | Includes bibliographical references.
Identifiers: LCCN 2017049881 | ISBN 9781611806229 (pbk.: alk. paper)
Subjects: LCSH: Mysticism—History—Middle Ages, 600–1500.
Classification: LCC BV5082.3 .C58 2018 | DDC 248.2/2—dc23
LC record available at https://lccn.loc.gov/2017049881

Whoever you are,
looking for peace,
this book is for you.

Contemplation is not the pleasant reaction to a celestial sunset, nor is it the perpetual twitter of heavenly birdsong. It is not even an emotion. It is the awareness of God, known and loved at the core of one's being.

—*Clifton Wolters*

If you can sit and do nothing, then you can do virtually anything.

—*Michael Elliston*

So less thinking and more loving.

—*William Johnston*

CONTENTS

ACKNOWLEDGMENTS

Thank you, Anonymous, for writing a text that makes reading an encounter with Mystery. Perennial gratitude to Dave O'Neal, senior editor at Shambhala, for creating this book—its *sine quo non*. Thank you, Ben Gleason, for contributing excellence in copyediting and project management, and thanks, Emily Coughlin, for shepherding this Shambhala Pocket Library edition into the world. Guyeth Nash is thanked for being there. Appreciation to Cynthia Bourgeault for her work and presence one frosty February weekend at the Conyers monastery a month before Anonymous had his masterpiece released into the twenty-first century, for her liking my translation made me feel an exam had been passed and I could stay in school. Thankfulness to publishing maven Lil Copan for generously sharing insights and her willingness to listen. Decades of gratitude to John Algeo, mentor and Professor Emeritus of English at The University of Georgia, ever mindful that he taught me translation as I cut my teeth on Ælfric's Old English manuscripts. Praise to James Patrick Cronin for his dedication to his craft and superlative narration of the *Cloud* that would surprise and please its medieval author. For my wonderful colleagues in the College Writing Programs at Berkeley and for my students there and elsewhere, thank you for community. Last, for appreciation of sunshine no one out-naps Lucky, now fifteen and still contributing perfect tranquility to our days. And for those I love *with al myn herte in hole entente*—Sean, Kate, John—thank you like a snowy egret rising from the marsh.

CARMEN ACEVEDO BUTCHER
University of California, Berkeley

INTRODUCTION

This book you now hold is a rainmaker for anyone whose soul has ever felt as dry as a bone. Its nameless author was a gifted teacher. Page after page, he patiently explains what contemplative prayer is and how it can end any spiritual drought—shortages of love, low levels of humility, an absence of peace. Through practical spiritual exercises that he calls the "cloud of unknowing" and the "cloud of forgetting," he teaches us to pray without ceasing and shows us that a dialogue with Mystery is not only possible but is in fact "the work of the soul that most pleases God."[1]

Anonymous begins with a call to self-examination and humility, then recommends contemplative prayer as the only discipline that can deeply purify the soul.[2] He describes it as "the easiest work of all, when a soul is helped by grace,"[3] and gives us this advice: "So stop hesitating. Do this work until you feel the delight of it. In the trying is the desire."[4]

Next, Anonymous explains what he means by "the cloud of unknowing," and how this prayer helps us silence our analytical minds, freeing our hearts to love.

An experienced mystic, our author understands that contemplative prayer does not immediately enlighten. He admits, in fact, that it may seem like the most unilluminated place, initially:

> The first time you practice contemplation, you'll only experience a darkness, like a cloud of unknowing. You won't know what this is. You'll only know that in your will you feel a simple reaching out to God. You must also know that this darkness and this cloud will always be between you and your God, whatever you do. They will always keep you from seeing him clearly by the light of understanding in your intellect and will block you from feeling him fully in the sweetness of love in your emotions. So, be sure you make your home in this darkness.[5]

He writes as one who has mastered this early stage but who remembers its uncertainty and worry. He keeps reassuring us that we need only one thing: *a nakid entent* ("a naked intent"),[6] a "simple reaching out" to God that is this "cloud of unknowing." Contemplation requires us to be still, if we want to get acquainted with its discipline, because God cannot be grasped with our minds, only by our love, as Jesus told the curious, well-educated lawyer: "Love the Lord your God with all your heart, soul, and mind, and your neighbor as yourself."[7]

Anonymous makes this same point when he teaches us that "we can't think our way to God," saying, "That's why I'm willing to abandon everything I know, to love the one thing I cannot think. He can be loved, but not thought."[8]

Then he describes the second necessity for contemplative prayer—a kind of spiritual amnesia:

> To the cloud of unknowing above you and between you and your God, add the cloud of forgetting beneath you, between you and creation. If the cloud of unknowing makes you feel alienated from God, that's only because you've not yet put a cloud of forgetting between you and everything in creation. When I say "everything in creation," I mean not only the creatures themselves but also everything they do and are, as well as the circumstances in which they find themselves. There are no exceptions. You must forget everything. Hide all created things, material and spiritual, good and bad, under the cloud of forgetting.[9]

Anonymous offers timeless practical advice that we as readers seek as we come to the *Cloud* to learn about prayer. For example, he recommends that we focus our scattered minds on one small word and try to hold on to it:

Select a little word of one syllable, not two. The shorter the word, the more it helps the work of the spirit. *God* or *love* works well. Pick one of these or any other word you like, as long as it is one syllable. Fasten it to your heart. Fix your mind on it permanently, so nothing can dislodge it.[10]

He teaches that such contemplation reconnects us to God: "If humanity had never sinned, this work would not have stopped."[11] A wise mentor, he says that if we choose to contemplate the word *sin*, saturating our souls with it, we will learn "how large every sin is because even the smallest sin separates us from God and prevents us from knowing true peace of soul."[12]

Above all, his books are encouraging. Their anonymous author reassures us often, saying: "You only need a naked intent for God. When you long for him, that's enough."[13] He develops this idea in many down-to-earth ways, helping us enter into a deeper understanding of God as we experience the purity of contemplative prayer.

A Shilling in the Armpit

The Cloud of Unknowing was written in England sometime during the last half of the fourteenth century, an age of pandemic. The bubonic plague reached the island in 1348, raged through 1349, reappeared several more times before century's end, and returned haphazardly for hundreds of years. The horror is heard in a medieval Welsh lament: "Death invades us like black smoke! We fear the shilling in the armpit!"[14] This "shilling" was a chilling first symptom of the plague, an odd black swelling in the armpit or groin, followed by purple-black blotches covering the skin, violent vomiting, agonizing pain, and then death. Most victims were gone in under five days; others lasted less than twenty-four hours.

Millions caught it. Roughly half of England's population died.[15] Meanwhile, compassion suffered a slow death also. Guy de Chauliac, the well-known fourteenth-century physician to popes, observed that the deadly illness destroyed community: "Charity is dead."[16] In the introduction of the *Decameron*, Giovanni Boccaccio describes the inhumanity of that time:

> Neighbors never helped neighbors, and even relatives shunned each other. Brother deserted brother, uncle left nephew, sister forgot brother, and sometimes wife neglected husband. Worst of all, parents abandoned their children, as if they didn't know them.[17]

The plague was merely one of the fourteenth century's difficulties. From 1337 on, England was also at war with France during the 116 years of the on-again, off-again (and numerically mislabeled) "Hundred Years' War," while the Peasants' Revolt began in the summer of 1381 after yet another unfair poll tax sparked social unrest. Commoners grabbed rusty swords, scythes, and axes and stormed their way through the counties of Essex and Kent, opening prisons, attacking monasteries, sacking stately manors, killing every lawyer they could find, and burning whatever they could get their hands on.[18]

The ugly fourteenth century was also the prelude to the Great Reformation. Why did Martin Luther nail his *Ninety-Five Theses* and the flaws of Catholicism to the Wittenberg Castle Church door on October 31, 1517? For starters, the corrupt Avignon Papacy (1309–1377) had damaged the Catholic Church. Seven secularized French popes—Clement V, John XXII, Benedict XII, Clement VI, Innocent VI, Urban V, and Gregory XI—took up residence in Avignon and worshipped opulence, ate from golden plates, fought expensive wars, and meddled in politics instead of feeding the poor and following Christ. Pope Gregory XI brought the papacy back to Rome seventy years later in 1378, but the politically driven Western Schism started four more decades of ecclesiastical in-fighting, resolved by the Council of Constance in 1417. Add to these "holy wars" Johannes Gutenberg's mid-fifteenth-century printing press and the Bibles, other books, and documents it produced—including Luther's *Ninety-Five Theses*—and suddenly you have a more well-informed populace, many of whom would not indulge their leaders in anything less than the uncorrupted truth.

During Worldly Storms, Mystic Calm

Out of plague, ego-triggered wars, social inequality and disorder, a divided Church, and technological change came England's devotional classics, as never before and never since. English mysticism took root in the confusion of transition and grew in the vernacular works of Walter Hilton, Julian of Norwich, Richard Rolle, and the *Cloud*'s Anonymous. English—Middle English, to be precise—was used for the first time instead of the less-accessible Latin to lead those with restless hearts into an ancient peace.[19] What was true for the island was also true for Europe. Birgitta of Sweden, Angela de Foligno, Beatrijs of Nazareth, Catherine of Siena, Meister Johannes Eckhart, Gertrude the Great, Thomas à Kempis, Marguerite d'Oingt, Marguerite Porete, Mechthild of Hackeborn, Mechthild of Magdeburg, and Umiltà of Faenza are some of the continental mystics who wrote during this turbulent but fruitful period.[20]

These writers teach "contemplation" as a practical spiritual exercise that, through grace, unites an individual's soul with God.[21] Their goal is audacious—nothing short of total union with the Creator and Savior. They teach contemplation as a spiritual craft that can be learned by anyone, the way cooking or writing can be mastered, if you are dedicated. This outbreak of devotional literature has one theme: contemplation is synonymous with God's love. It creates interior peace and exterior acts of kindness that Catholics call "good works" and Protestants call "service to the Lord."

As the fourteenth century came to a close, Hilton, Julian, Chaucer, and the *Cloud*'s author were all writing at the same time. The English language was alive in new ways in their hands, and the *Cloud*'s Anonymous contributed to this flowering of mysticism with seven widely circulated works of English prose. He authored four of these—*The Cloud of Unknowing*, *An Epistle on Prayer*, *Discretion of Stirrings*, and *The Book of Privy Counsel*, and he adapted three—Pseudo-Dionysius the Areopagite's *Mystical Theology,* Richard of St. Victor's *Twelve Patriarchs* (or *Benjamin Minor*), and two of St. Bernard's sermons on the Song of Songs.[22]

The Mystery of the Non-Self-Promoting Author

Who was the author of this masterpiece? Scholars have tried and failed to identify him, but his writings reveal an outspoken, strong-willed, wise, likable, exceptionally articulate, and caring teacher whom we would all like to meet. He is both bright and down-to-earth and, best of all, his descriptions of contemplation show that he is writing from experience, as we see when he compares contemplative prayer to sleep:

> When we're asleep, the functions of our physical faculties are suspended so our bodies can get complete

rest. Sleep nourishes and strengthens our bodies in every way. The same is true of the spiritual "sleep" of contemplative prayer. The stubborn questions of our restless spirituality and of all our creative and rational thoughts are firmly bound and totally emptied, so the happy soul can sleep soundly, resting profoundly in the loving awareness of God as he is, completely nourished and strengthened in spirit.[23]

Short of some unexpected manuscript or archaeological discovery, the name of this unforgettable author is destined to remain unknown, just as he wished. Although his works were popular in their day—often copied on vellum and distributed from monastery to monastery to great house—he chose to keep his identity private even then. This anonymity is, however, appropriate for someone whose main goal was to advance God's love. Human praise did not matter to him, and his personal obscurity is synonymous with his main message: Christ should become more visible as his followers become humbler and kinder (and less obvious).

We can guess that he may have been a priest. The ecclesiastical prayers and blessings at the beginning and end of the *Cloud* suggest this possibility, but he may have also been a monk, perhaps a Carthusian, because that order focuses on Christian mysticism and is known for its austere discipline.

The dialect of his language helps us locate him in England's East Midland area,[24] near another famous spiritual author, Walter Hilton, who wrote *The Ladder of Perfection* in the same East Midland dialect. Hilton was a fourteenth-century Augustinian mystic living in Newark-on-Trent, in the East Midlands area of Nottinghamshire, so perhaps he and the *Cloud* author were close enough to visit each other often.

Like the sixth-century Benedict of Nursia, for whom we have so few personal details but who left us his eternally wise, gently challenging *Rule,* this unidentified medieval author comes to us clouded by anonymity but with his extraordinary personality preserved in his prose. When we read these ancient works, it is easy to believe that their uniquely engaging, humbly wise language could only come from the styli of people we wish we could have met.

The Work's Twenty-Something Audience

Part of the charisma of the *Cloud* is its personal tone. We feel as if we are overhearing one side of a private chat between friends. Obviously Anonymous is writing to someone he knows well. Equally anonymous, this unknown friend is twenty-four at the time of the *Cloud*'s creation (the one solid fact we have about either author or audience). The tone is that of an affectionate dialogue. It is animated and intimate. We expect such a tone between those who know each other well in a student-teacher or novice-spiritual director relationship.

We see this dynamic familiarity in the way that Anonymous gives his student an unvarnished warning about not wasting time: "We only get the present moment. . . . Time is made for us; we're not made for time. . . . [And] none of us has an excuse on Judgment Day when we go before God to give an account of how we spent our time."[25] Mentors chronically give this advice to those younger than they are, and it is bound to chafe. But Anonymous knows this and does not move at once to the next topic. Instead, he follows up with a bold anticipation of the objections that his spiritual apprentice must have, saying:

> I can hear you complaining: "What am I supposed to do then? I know you're right, but how can I give an itemized account of each moment? I'm twenty-four already. I never noticed time before. Your argument has already convinced me there's no way I can go back in time and change things. Time doesn't work that way, nor does ordinary grace. I can't go back in time and make amends."[26]

Although this young student is unknown, he was most likely associated with a monastery. In what way is hard to say. Today, monasticism is more clearly defined than it was in the Middle Ages. In the late fourteenth century, the *Cloud* could have been written to a layperson, such as a nobleman who had made a general commitment to the monastic life (called the *propositum*). We will never know for sure.

Positive Use of the Negative Way

While the *Cloud* author leans on the mystical tradition of others who came before him, he does so (as he does everything) in a wholly original fashion. One of these sources is Pseudo-Dionysius the Areopagite, simply called "Dionysius" here. An anonymous monk and mystic, Dionysius is thought to have lived in Syria in the late fifth to early sixth century. He took the pseudonym of St. Paul's Athenian convert—"Dionysius the Areopagite" (Acts 17:34)—to give his writings more authority.[27] It worked. In the Middle Ages, from East to West, his writings were viewed with a quasi-apostolic authority.[28]

Dionysius wrote in Greek and was translated into Latin. His theme is that we can experience a union with God in this life only by "unknowing." We must abandon all thoughts and sensory perceptions and embrace a darkness in which we wait patiently for an illumination that may or may not come. This is the *via negativa*, or "negative way," and Dionysius attempts to describe God only in terms of what cannot be said about him. Knowing-by-not-knowing is also called *apophasis* because it describes what God is *not*. *Apophasis* is rooted in the

Greek *apophanai*, meaning "to not say," from *apo*, "not," and *phanai*, "to say." An apophatic approach to God literally means "to not say" or "to un-say" God.

The ninth-century Irish theologian John Scottus Eriugena, who translated and wrote commentaries on Dionysius, gives a classic definition of the *via negativa* taught by both this anonymous Syrian monk and our *Cloud* author: "Nothing can really be said about God. No single noun, verb, or any other part of speech can describe him. Why do we expect visible signs to be able to articulate the invisible nature of God?"[29] Dionysius admits the limits of words in the presence of Mystery: "What is to be said of it remains unsayable; what is to be understood of it remains unknowable."[30]

In this prayer from *Mystical Theology*, he articulates his apophatic approach:

> Trinity beyond all essence, all divinity, all goodness! Guide of Christians to divine wisdom, direct our path to the ultimate summit of your mystical lore, most incomprehensible, most luminous, and most exalted, where the pure, absolute, and immutable mysteries of theology are veiled in the dazzling obscurity of the secret silence, outshining all brilliance with the intensity of their darkness, and surcharging our blinded intellects with the utterly impalpable and invisible fairness of glories surpassing all beauty.[31]

In the *Cloud*, our anonymous author also recommends this way of not-knowing:

Become blind during contemplative prayer and cut yourself off from needing to know things. Knowledge hinders, not helps you in contemplation. Be content feeling moved in a delightful, loving way by something mysterious and unknown, leaving you focused entirely on God, with no other thought than of him alone. Let your naked desire rest there.[32]

Anonymous also turned the gold of his sources into platinum when he mined material from one twelfth-century writer in particular: Richard of St. Victor, whose reputation as a mystic was such that Dante singled him out for praise in the *Paradiso*, calling him "in contemplation more than human" (X, 132). Richard was a scholastic theologian and one of the first to articulate a step-by-step approach to teaching others contemplation. He was also a pioneer in analyzing the contemplative experience.[33] His work was shaped by the German mystic Hugo of St. Victor, and Richard served as prior of the Augustinian abbey of St. Victor in Paris from 1162 until his death in 1173. In *The Twelve Patriarchs*, *The Mystical Ark* (also called *Benjamin Major*), and *On the Trinity*, Richard's teaching is often Augustinian in its language of ascending to God through various stages and in the positive (kataphatic) terminology it uses to express God's identity, though it also has elements of the *via negativa*.

Richard of St. Victor understood that contemplation is a way of looking and an attitude of mind. *The Cloud of Unknowing* is steeped in his teaching: "Contemplation is the free, more penetrating gaze of a mind, suspended with wonder,"[34] Richard explains in his *Mystical Ark*. Distinguishing between thinking, meditating, and contemplation, he says that thinking is a rambling analysis of many things, a truth John Keats observes in "Ode to a Nightingale" when he writes that "the dull brain perplexes and retards"; while meditation is a mental activity focused on one thing, the gaining of knowledge; and contemplation—because it is not a mental process— surpasses both.[35]

Richard was followed in the thirteenth century by the last great teacher of the school of St. Victor, Thomas Gallus. Gallus fused apophatic mysticism with an affective reading of the Song of Songs to teach the "superior wisdom" of the human heart over intellect, urging readers to listen for the voice of the Beloved with the "ears of experience."[36] This view profoundly influenced the *Cloud* author, whose goal on every page is an echo of Gregory the Great's well-known phrase, "Love itself is a kind of knowing."[37]

The resonance that our anonymous author must have felt with the teachers of the school of St. Victor especially shows in chapters 62 through 66 of the *Cloud*, when he discusses the spiritual meanings of ordinary contemplative terms. His definitions of reason, will, imagination, and the five senses show the influence of Hugo, Richard, and Thomas Gallus.[38] The *Cloud* author also adopts Richard's symbolic interpretation of the Ark of the Covenant, and he presents it with an originality demonstrating the warm relationship between him and the disciple to whom he is writing. Anonymous honors and encourages his student by identifying him with Aaron, the priestly keeper of the Ark, while comparing himself to Bezalel, the maker of the Ark. In doing so, he personalizes these metaphors and lets his disciple know of his faith in him:[39]

So, spiritual friend, though my writing is as simple as a child's and incompetent and though I'm certainly the worst teacher you can imagine, not worthy to instruct anyone, I bear the office of Bezalel, creating and making plain for you the nature of this spiritual Ark. Here, I put it in your hands. And you can do far better than I, if you'll be Aaron. Dedicate yourself to gazing on the Ark of contemplation without ceasing, for both of us. Do this, please, for the love of God Almighty.[40]

The Ancient Medicine of Contemplation

The *Cloud* is also a part of the ancient tradition of Christian contemplative wisdom, which has come a long way from the dust of Egypt and the Desert Mothers and Fathers who were among the first to practice it, as well as the earliest Benedictines who dedicated themselves daily to regular times of *lectio divina*, or deliberate, mindful "sacred reading." The largely *via negativa* approach of contemplation was advanced in Spain in the sixteenth century by John of the Cross and Teresa of Avila. In language our *Cloud* author would have recognized, John of the Cross describes the "darkness" of contemplation and its ability to purify us and teach us how to love:

[The soul] departed on a dark night, attracted by God and enkindled with love for him alone. This dark night is a privation and purgation of all sensible appetites for the external things of the world, the delights of the flesh, and the gratifications of the will. . . . For love effects a likeness between the lover and the loved.[41]

Teresa of Avila also prayed contemplatively. She called it "the prayer of quiet" and experienced its power for reviving a "desolate and very dry" heart, leading the "servants of love" to a union with God that is like "rain that comes down abundantly from heaven to soak and saturate the whole garden [of the soul]."[42]

In the twentieth century, contemplation found expression in the practice of centering (or listening) prayer taught by Trappist monks such as Thomas Keating, still much read today. The British poet T. S. Eliot also followed in the contemplative footsteps of the anonymous *Cloud* author. In the writings of Evelyn Underhill and others, Eliot found meditation a way of tapping into the mysteries of poetry, and his works resonate with the preoccupations of our *Cloud* author. In *East Coker*, Eliot writes: "In order to arrive at what you do not know / You must go by a way which is the way of ignorance. . . . And what you do not know is the only thing you know." Contemplation's vibrant presence continues to be felt today, for example, in the work of the Quaker Richard Foster and of the Benedictine sister Joan Chittister.

Why has contemplation endured over the centuries? Perhaps the answer is as simple as "plain old death," as Kurt Vonnegut observed. We wake up many mornings with the creepy certainty that one day, perhaps this very day, will be our last on earth, as Vonnegut described our common mortality in chapter 1 of *Slaughterhouse-Five*: "And even if wars didn't keep coming like glaciers, there would still be plain old death." Also, perhaps contemplation has endured because we need its profound peace to battle the isolation that selfishness and plain old stupidity bring. We all make mistakes. And we hunger for the ancient wisdom found in *The Cloud of Unknowing* because it builds bridges and works for social justice. It teaches us how to love, grow up, be fully human.

We need contemplation because, as our globe gets more crowded by the hour, more and more we act like elbow-to-elbow passengers in cheap coach seats on a commuter flight. We jostle for an inch more room and feel our faces heat up when someone gets our cargo space. To escape, we plunk ourselves down each day in front of the virtual infinity offered by computer screens and rarely stand under the sky and stare at the stars. Technology moves at the speed of sound, and we all struggle to keep up with current events and the latest social media platforms. Who doesn't rush through the day? Who never feels the pressure to produce? How often are you in cyberspace? Our new frantic pace is like poison to our holding hands with those we love.

That is where contemplation comes in. It reconnects us to ourselves, to God, and to others. It helps us learn to forgive and heal our souls, an action as basic as washing our hands or studying the ABCs in kindergarten. As Daniel Goleman says, meditation is "an antidote to the mind's vulnerability to toxic emotions."[43] Simply put, we need a way to generate joy. In a University of Wisconsin lab during the summer of 2001, a few months before 9/11, a Tibetan Buddhist monk submitted to the experiment of having his brain waves monitored by an EEG, and as he meditated, the results were remarkable. When the monk began contemplating in a way designed to nurture compassion within himself, the EEG sensors registered an actual shift—to a state of joy.[44]

For the first sixteen centuries of the Christian church, contemplative prayer was *the* goal of Christian spirituality, and now in our own time of transition and upheaval, five hundred years after the Great Reformation, we are returning to our roots. Contemplative prayer is more relevant than ever before. More and more of us are practicing this ancient form of prayer and finding peace in a world of war, extreme political divide, epidemics, terrorism, technology, overcrowding, noise, inequality, and a Church in need of humility.

Not Translating Word-for-Word but Sense-by-Sense

My translation tries to articulate the intimacy between the *Cloud* writer and his audience. As always, I stay as close to the original as possible, gently transforming it, pass after pass, into the English we speak today. I also want irresistible prose. This may sound far-fetched when discussing a book of devotional literature, but it is a requirement in my mind, because the original text is simply beautiful. To be true to this Middle English prose, I have to imitate its "pull." So I snub obsolete, antiquated diction, not wanting to bore the intelligent reader, and I don't choose two words if one will do. This simplicity would have pleased our medieval author.

I also refuse a blow-by-blow translation. That is the definition of a "crib," and others have already done this. Yes, cribs are helpful to the student of medieval literature, but word-for-word translations are not read for pleasure. They are wooden. Only a sense-by-sense interpretation makes you want to pick a book up over and over again. Every translation is interpretation, and even though that term makes me cringe, moving ideas from one language to another is not an act of duplication. A different but faithful version is created by listening keenly and humbly to the original's voice.

Therefore, my translation is gender-inclusive on purpose, the way that Barry Patrick, O.S.B., transformed the masculine language of Benedict's *Rule* in 1997. I thought that a book on love should cast as wide a net as possible. Different translators handle this linguistic challenge in diverse ways. Some choose "men and women" when the author means "humanity," but this phrase does eventually get awkward. The reader would have to juggle too many pairings like "he and she" and "him and her" and so on. My solution is to use "you" a little more often than it presents itself in the text. This technique suits the book's epistolary nature. Sometimes I also use "they" with a singular antecedent, as Jane Austen, Shakespeare, and Lewis Carroll did in novels and plays. This is sure to annoy teachers of English who wear grammar collars, but I hope it appeals to everyone else.

Divided into seventy-five chapters (or letters), the *Cloud* teaches the basics of contemplative prayer in a personal, feeling way. As a guide for readers, I created endnotes in the same spirit that I would add a "PS" at the end of a letter to a friend. These notes enlighten in often surprising, fun ways, parting the curtain between our postmodern world and the Middle Ages. They provide useful historical background, such as the gruesome effects of the black plague, our author's understanding of atoms, and the meaning of medieval Christian symbols. They also help readers enter the deeply medieval and monastic way of understanding words. One note reveals that our anonymous author's *entent* ("intent")—to help us stretch our minds toward God in contemplation and grow spiritually—has much in common with our words *intense*, *tendon*, *attention*, *attend*, *attentive*, and *extend*. (They all share the Latin root for "to stretch.") These notes also give the reader the opportunity to compare the original Middle English texts with their modern translations. One delves into the verb "to help," finding its history in the Middle English verb, *holpen*, still heard in Appalachia and elsewhere, though it's fast disappearing. I am particularly fond of this linguistic fossil because I grew up with my kind neighbors asking me in various ways, "Can I holp?"

In these notes, we also hear from the best contemporary and ancient minds, from the Desert Fathers and Mothers to Christian mysticism scholars like Bernard McGinn and Ursula King to the American authors Ralph Waldo Emerson and Joan Didion, all discussing truth, love, and contemplative prayer. Readers dipping into the endnotes will find themselves amply rewarded, over and over.

Finally, to read the Middle English *Cloud of Unknowing* is to practice contemplation. Our ingenious anonymous author planned it that way. He is an accomplished rhetorician, and his mimetic style is no accident. In my own limited way, I have tried to imitate the exercise of contemplative prayer in this book, but if you want to taste it fully, google Patrick J. Gallacher's online edition of the *Cloud* and a good online Middle English dictionary, brush up on Chaucer's English, and dare to read the *Cloud* master on his own turf.[45]

THE CLOUD OF UNKNOWING

This book of contemplation, called *The Cloud of Unknowing,* begins here and shows you how to unite your soul with God.

Prayer for the Preface

God, to you all hearts are open, to you all longings speak, and to you no secret thing is hidden. I beg you—purify the intentions[1] of my heart through the unspeakable[2] gift of your grace, so I can love you with all I am and praise you for all you are. Amen.

PREFACE

In the name of the Father and of the Son and of the Holy Spirit.

And in the name of love, I ask you, whoever you are, however this book came into your hands—maybe you own it, have borrowed it, are delivering it to someone else, or are safekeeping it for others—regardless, I beg you in the powerful name of love, if at all possible don't read it to anyone or copy it or quote from it, and don't let anyone else read it, copy it, or quote from it, unless, in your opinion, that person is sincere in their intentions to follow Christ.[1] They must be ready to go to the next level, advancing beyond the active life[2] to the highest contemplative life. Grace takes us there in this present world through purity of soul, even though our bodies are mortal. Entrust this book only to those who for a long time have been doing everything possible in prayer and virtuous living to prepare themselves for the contemplative journey; otherwise, this book is not for them.

I also ask in the name of love that you accept some advice from me and please pass this advice on to others who read, copy, quote, or listen to this book. Promise me that you'll take the time to read it all the way through, and ask them to do this, too. Here's why. What if you find something at the beginning of the book, or halfway through that makes you question why a point was left hanging or wasn't clarified in more detail? But in later chapters the point is completely explained, if only you had read the very next chapter or one at the end of the book. That's how a person who reads one section but not another could be led into error.[3] It would be so easy. To avoid this spiritual misstep and to help others avoid it, too, I'm asking you— please do what I say, for love.

I hope that habitual gossips, boasters, flatterers, fault-finders, busybodies, whisperers, liars, and character assassinators never see this book.[4] I never meant to write anything for them. I don't want them meddling in these matters, nor do I want the merely curious, educated or uneducated,[5] prying into this subject. Even if they're good people with active lives, it will mean nothing to them, unless they're also inwardly stirred by God's mysterious Spirit, allowing them to participate in contemplation at the highest level from time to time. Then, through God's grace, even if they can't do this work unceasingly, as true contemplatives can, they'll find that this book will go a long way in strengthening and comforting them in all they do.

This book has seventy-five chapters. The last one discusses what signs to look for if you want to know whether or not God has called you to do the work of contemplation.

Dear spiritual friend in God, examine your life. Pay careful attention to the way you live out your calling. With all your heart, thank God for your blessings, and his grace will help you stand strong in the face of subtle attacks from within and without, until you win the everlasting crown of life. Amen.

1

The four stages of the Christian life,
and how the disciple for whom this book
was written advanced in this calling

Dear spiritual friend in God, I want to tell you what my humble searching has found true about growing as a Christian. You'll experience four stages of maturity that I call the *ordinary,* the *special,* the *singular,* and the *perfect.*[1] You can begin and complete the first three stages in this earthly life. Grace will help you start the fourth here also, but it will last forever in the heavenly joy of eternity. You will notice these stages are listed in this order: first, the *ordinary,* then the *special,* next the *singular,* and last, the *perfect.*[2] Our Lord in his profound mercy has called you to progress through them in this order, leading you by the desires of your heart.[3]

You remember the first stage. You lived the *ordinary* Christian life with your friends out in the world, until God's eternal love could no longer stand your being so far from him, because first he created you from nothing and later he paid his priceless blood for you when you followed Adam and got lost. So, with an irresistible kindness, he nudged your desire awake, fastened it to a leash[4] of longing, and led you to the next level, so you could be his servant, serving those he loves.[5] At this *special* level, he knew you would learn to live more abundantly and more spiritually than you had before.

What else did he do? He didn't abandon you at that stage, because he loves you with all of his heart. He's loved you since you began. So what did he do next? See how forcefully and how gently he pulled[6] you to the third level, the *singular*? Along this solitary way, you'll learn to lift up the foot of your love[7] and walk in kindness toward purity. This fourth, *perfect* level is the final one.

2

---

*A short lesson on humility and
the work of contemplation*

Cheer up. Yes, you're weak. And, yes, life is hard.
Accept this, and then take a good hard look at yourself.
Who are you? What have you done to deserve being
called by our Lord to this work? Is anyone's heart so
fast asleep in laziness, so worn-out and miserable, that
it isn't jolted awake by the pull of this love and the
sound of his voice calling? You're human, so watch out
for that enemy, pride. Never think you're holier or
better than anyone else. Never confuse the worthiness
of your calling with who you are. Don't think that, just
because you're at the third, or *singular* level, you're
more important than others. In fact, if you don't live
out your calling, empowered by grace and good advice,
the opposite will be true. You'll be worse off, more
miserable and cut off from community than you can
imagine. So let grace and wise instruction lead you to
the good in your soul and then act on that good.

Live up to your high calling by lowering yourself. Become more loving to your spiritual partner, never forgetting how he—almighty God, King of Kings, and Lord of Lords—chose to humble himself for you. He was so compassionate that he chose you from among his flock of sheep as one of his special disciples. He put you in his pasture to eat the sweetness of his love, letting you sample your eternal, heavenly inheritance.

Continue doing what's right. Be strong. Look forward and let go of what happened yesterday. Look at your weaknesses, not at your strengths, and pay attention to what you still need to do, instead of rehearsing in your mind what you've already accomplished. This is the best way to get and keep humility. Every aspect of your life must be founded on holy desires, if you're going to advance along the way of purity. In every possible way, turn your will over to God's all-powerful hand.

I especially want you to remember this: God is a jealous lover. He will not share you, so don't give yourself to anyone but him. He's unwilling to work in your will unless you're willing to be entirely his, and his alone. He's not asking for your help. He's asking for you. He wants you to lock[1] your eyes on him and leave him alone to work in you. Your part is to protect the door and windows, keeping out intruders and flies.[2] And if you're willing to do that, just ask him, praying humbly, and he will help you immediately.

So pray. And let's see how you do. God is completely ready. He's only waiting on you. What will you do? Where will you begin?

3

---

*How to do the work of contemplation,
and why it is the best work*

Lift up your heart to God[1] with a gentle stirring[2] of love. Focus on him alone. Want him, and not anything he's made. Think on nothing but him. Don't let anything else run through your mind and will. Here's how. Forget what you know. Forget everything God made and everybody who exists and everything that's going on in the world, until your thoughts and emotions aren't focused on or reaching[3] toward anything, not in a general way and not in any particular way. Let them be. For the moment, don't care about anything.

This is the work[4] of the soul that most pleases God. All saints and angels rejoice in it, and they're always willing to help you when you're spending time in contemplation. They rush to your side, their powers ready. But contemplation infuriates the devil and his company. That's why they try to stop you in any way they can. Everyone on earth has been helped by contemplation in wonderful ways. You can't know how much. This spiritual exercise even lessens the pain for souls in purgatory. And no other discipline can purify your soul as deeply or make you as virtuous. But it's the easiest work of all, when a soul is helped by grace to feel a pure desire—contemplation follows. Otherwise, it's hard, nearly impossible to do.

So stop hesitating. Do this work until you feel the delight of it. In the trying is the desire. The first time you practice contemplation, you'll only experience a darkness, like a cloud of unknowing.[5] You won't know what this is. You'll only know that in your will you feel a simple reaching out to God.[6] You must also know that this darkness and this cloud will always be between you and your God, whatever you do. They will always keep you from seeing him clearly by the light of understanding in your intellect and will block you from feeling him fully in the sweetness of love in your emotions. So, be sure you make your home in this darkness. Stay there as long as you can, crying out to him over and over again, because you love him. It's the closest you can get to God here on earth, by waiting in this darkness and in this cloud. Work at this diligently, as I've asked you to, and I know God's mercy will lead you there.

4

_____

Contemplation's brevity, and why knowledge and
imagination can't acquire it

_____ ·

So you won't go down the wrong path in this work,[1]
thinking contemplation is something it's not, I'll tell
you more about it. Some people believe contemplation
is time-consuming, but it's not. In fact, it takes less
time than anything else you'll ever do. It's as brief as
an atom,[2] which excellent philosophers in the science
of astronomy define as the smallest particle of time. An
atom's littleness[3] makes it indivisible, nearly inconceiv-
able, and also invaluable. On this subject, it has been
written, "Every moment of time is a gift to you, and
one day you'll be asked how you spent each one."[4] And
you should be held responsible for it, because this brief-
est moment of time is exactly how long it takes your
will, that strong architect of your soul, to desire something and to act on that desire. In an hour, you experience the same number of aspirations and cravings as
there are atoms in that space of time, and if you were
restored by grace to the original purity of your soul,

you'd be the master of every impulse. You'd never feel out of control, because your every desire would be directed toward the most desirable and highest good, who is God.[5]

He measures us and makes his divinity fit our souls, and our souls are able to take the measure of him because he created us in his image and made us worthy. He alone is complete and can fulfill our every longing. God's grace restores our souls and teaches us how to comprehend him through love. He is incomprehensible to the intellect. Even angels know him by loving him. Nobody's mind is powerful enough to grasp who God is. We can only know him by experiencing his love.

Look. Every rational creature, every person, and every angel has two main strengths: the power to know and the power to love. God made both of these, but he's not knowable through the first one. To the power of love, however, he is entirely known, because a loving soul is open to receive God's abundance. Each person loves uniquely, and God's limitlessness can fill all angels and all souls that will ever exist. His very nature makes love endless and miraculous. God will never stop loving us. Consider this truth, and, if by grace you can make love your own, do. For the experience is eternal joy; its absence is unending suffering.

If you were changed enough by God's grace, you could continue controlling the unceasing and inherent impulses of your will, and by succeeding in this exercise here on earth, you'd never be without a taste of the eternal sweetness, and, later, in the joy of heaven, you'd never be without every food. So don't be surprised if I direct you to the work of contemplation. If humanity had never sinned, this work would not have stopped. You were made for contemplation, and everything in the universe conspires to help you with it. And contemplation will heal you. I'll tell you more about this subject later. The person who shirks this exercise falls deeper and deeper into sin, moving further and further from God, but the one who practices this discipline rises higher and higher above sin, drawing nearer and nearer to God.

So take good care of your time. Watch how you spend it, for nothing is more precious. In the twinkling of an eye, heaven can be won or lost. Here's how we know time is precious. God, the giver of time, never gives us two moments simultaneously; instead, he gives them to us one after another. We never get the future. We only get the present moment. He does this to establish order in his creation and to keep cause and effect in place. Time is made for us; we're not made for time.[6] God is the ruler of nature, but his gift of time has no strings attached—it never determines our own nature and natural impulses. Instead, each of these exactly corresponds to one atom of time. That way, none of us has an excuse on Judgment Day when we go before God to give an account of how we spent our time. We won't be able to say, "You gave me two moments at once to my every single impulse."

I can hear you complaining: "What am I supposed to do then? I know you're right, but how can I give an itemized account of each moment? I'm twenty-four already. I never noticed time before. Your argument has already convinced me there's no way I can go back in time and change things. Time doesn't work that way, nor does ordinary grace. I can't go back in time and make amends. I'm also well aware that because I'm weak and slow about some things spiritually, I can no more control the time to come than I did the time past. At best, I'll manage maybe one out of a hundred impulses well. So tell me what to do. Help me now, for the love of Jesus."

It is good that you said, "for the love of Jesus." For in the love of Jesus you'll find your help. Love is so powerful that it shares everything. So love Jesus, and everything he has will be yours. Through his divinity, he is the maker and giver of time, and through his humanity, he is the true keeper of time. His divinity and his humanity combined make him the best judge, the one most qualified to question how we've spent our time. Cling to him in love and in faith, and through that powerful bonding, you'll become his companion. His friends will be your friends. By "friends," I mean our Lady, St. Mary, who was full of grace and made the most of her time; the heavenly angels, who never waste time;[7] and the saints in heaven and on earth, who by the grace of Jesus and through the power of love make best use of their time.

See? This truth will comfort you and give you strength. Think clearly about what I've said, and your soul will grow. I do want to warn you about one thing in particular. I don't believe anyone can have a fellowship with Jesus, his holy Mother, the angels on high, and his saints, if that person doesn't make the effort to understand and appreciate time, with the help of grace. No matter how small the contribution, every person must work to strengthen the fellowship, as it does them.

Start practicing contemplation and watch how this spiritual exercise makes a difference in your life. When contemplation is genuine, it's nothing but a sudden impulse coming out of nowhere and flying up to God like a spark from a burning coal.[8] It's awesome to count how many times your soul stirs like that in an hour, but, of these, you may only have one instance when you suddenly realize you've completely forgotten every attachment you have on earth. You'll also notice that, because of our human frailty, each impulse rising to God immediately falls to earth in the form of a thought about something you've done or something that is still on your list to do. But so what? Right after that, it rises up again as fast as it did before.

See how it works? Contemplation is quite different from daydreaming or a delusion or a strange superstition. These don't come from a sincere and humble blind stirring of love, but from an arrogant, curious, and over-imaginative mind. The self-important, hyper-analytical intellect must always and in every way be squashed. Stomp it under foot, if you want to do the work of contemplation with integrity.

A person hearing this book read or quoted may misunderstand my point. I'm not saying that if a person thinks hard enough, he or she will succeed in the work of contemplation. I do not want people sitting around analyzing, racking their brains, their curiosity forcing their imagination to go entirely the wrong way. It's not natural. It's not wise for the mind, and it's not healthy for the body. These people are dangerously deluded, and it would take a miracle to save them. God in his infinite goodness and mercy would have to intervene, making these people stop such a wrong-minded approach and seek the counsel of experienced contemplatives; otherwise, such erring souls could succumb to madness, frenzied fits, or the devil's lies, which lead to the profound misery of sin and eventually to the loss of body and soul, for all eternity.

So, for the love of God, be careful in this work. Don't in any way approach contemplation with your intellect or your imagination. I'm telling you the truth—these won't help you. Leave them be and don't try to do the work of contemplation with them.

Also, don't get the wrong idea about my use of *darkness* and *cloud*. When I refer to this exercise as a darkness or a cloud, I don't want you to imagine the darkness that you get inside your house at night when you blow out a candle; nor do I want you to imagine a cloud crystallized from the moisture in the air. It's easy for your mind to picture either of these at any time. For example, even on the brightest, clearest summer day, you can imagine darkness or a cloud. Conversely, on the darkest night of winter, you can form a mental picture of a clear and shining light. They're not what I mean at all. Leave them alone. This way of thinking is nonsense.

When I say "darkness," I mean the absence of knowing. Whatever you don't know and whatever you've forgotten are "dark" to you, because you don't see them with your spiritual eyes. For the same reason, by "cloud" I don't mean a cloud in the sky, but a cloud of unknowing between you and God.

5

How contemplation requires us to hide
all people and all things past, present, and
future, and all accomplishments, under
the cloud of forgetting

If you ever want to make this cloud an integral part of
your life, so you can live and work[1] there, as I suggest,
you must do one more thing: complete the cloud of
unknowing with the cloud of forgetting. To the cloud
of unknowing above you and between you and your
God, add the cloud of forgetting beneath you, between
you and creation. If the cloud of unknowing makes you
feel alienated from God, that's only because you've not
yet put a cloud of forgetting between you and everything in creation. When I say "everything in creation,"
I mean not only the creatures themselves but also everything they do and are, as well as the circumstances
in which they find themselves. There are no exceptions.
You must forget everything. Hide all created things,

material and spiritual, good and bad, under the cloud of forgetting.

Obviously, sometimes it is helpful and even necessary to analyze situations and people, but the work of contemplation finds such analysis of little use. When you reflect on something going on or try to figure someone out, you're engaging in one type of spiritual vision—the eye of your soul opens and concentrates on an idea or person in the same way that an archer focuses on a target. However, as long as you're thinking about anything, it's above you, an obstacle between you and God, and the more you have in your mind that is not God, the further you are from him.

I also want to say with all due respect that when you're doing the work of contemplation it does you little good to focus on the kindness and importance of God, or on any of these: our Lady, the saints, angels, or the joys of heaven. Although you might think that approach would strengthen your purpose, it won't. Yes, we should remember God's kindness and love and praise him for our blessings, but it's much better to think on his naked being and to love and praise him for himself.

6

———

A short look at contemplation, through dialogue

———

I know you'll ask me, "How do I think on God as God, and who is God?" and I can only answer, "I don't know."

Your question takes me into the very darkness and cloud of unknowing that I want you to enter. We can know so many things. Through God's grace, our minds can explore, understand, and reflect on creation and even on God's own works, but we can't think our way to God. That's why I'm willing to abandon everything I know, to love the one thing I cannot think. He can be loved, but not thought. By love, God can be embraced and held, but not by thinking. It is good sometimes to meditate on God's amazing love as part of illumination and contemplation, but true contemplative work is something entirely different. Even meditating on God's love must be put down[1] and covered with a cloud of forgetting. Show your determination next. Let that joyful stirring of love make you resolute, and in its enthusiasm bravely step over meditation and reach up to penetrate the darkness above you. Then beat on that thick cloud of unknowing with the sharp arrow of longing and never stop loving, no matter what comes your way.

7

---

*How to deal with your thoughts during
contemplative prayer, especially when curiosity
and natural intelligence intrude*

Thoughts will come. If you find yourself obsessed with
one pressing down on you from above, trespassing between you and that darkness, and asking, "What are
you looking for? What do you want?" tell it that you
want only God—"I crave God. I seek him and nothing
else." If the thought persists, asking you who God is,
say that God is the One whose grace made you and
redeemed you and gave you this work, which is love.
Then add, "And you're in no position to understand
him. So sit back down.[1] Be still." For the love of God,
dismiss these thoughts,[2] even though they sound holy
and helpful.

You'll find thoughts seducing you in other ways. For
example, a thought may remind you of the many times
God has been kind to you and how he is amazingly
sweet and loving, full of grace and mercy. It[3] likes noth-

ing better than to grab your attention, and once it knows you're listening, the thought will start rambling. It will chatter on about Christ's Passion, drawing you in more and more, and then it will show you God's miraculous, sacrificial kindness. The thought loves you when you listen to it. Next, it will let you see how you used to live, when you were miserable and sinful, and as you begin thinking on those days, it will help you visualize where you lived at that time, and before you know it, your mind is scattered all over the place. How did this happen? You listened to the thought. You answered it, embraced it, and set it free.

Obviously these thoughts are good and holy, and they're required of anyone serious about contemplation. This is something of a paradox. For without countless sweet meditations on these very subjects— our agony, our shame, Christ's Passion, God's kindness, God's unfailing goodness, and God's worth—the contemplative person won't advance. But the man or woman experienced in these meditations must quit them. Put them down and hold them far under the cloud of forgetting, if you want to penetrate the cloud of unknowing between you and God.

So, when you feel drawn by grace to this work and decide to do it, lift your heart to him with a humble stirring of love. Focus on the God who made you and ransomed you and led you to this work. Think of nothing else. Even these thoughts are superfluous. Instead, do what pleases you. You only need a naked intent for God. When you long for him, that's enough.

If you want to gather this focus into one word, making it easier to grasp, select a little word of one syllable, not two. The shorter the word, the more it helps the work of the spirit. *God* or *love* works well. Pick one of these or any other word you like, as long as it is one syllable. Fasten it to your heart. Fix your mind on it permanently, so nothing can dislodge it.

This word will protect you. It will be your shield and spear, whether you ride out into peace or conflict.[4] Use it to beat on the dark cloud of unknowing above you. With it, knock down every thought, and they'll lie down under the cloud of forgetting below you. Whenever an idea interrupts you to ask, "What do you want?" answer with this one word. If the thought continues—if, for example, it offers out of its profound erudition to lecture you on your chosen word, expounding its etymology and connotations for you—tell it that you refuse to analyze the word, that you want your word whole, not broken into pieces. If you're able to stick to your purpose, I'm positive the thought will go away. Why? When you refuse to let it feed on the kinds of sweet meditations that we mentioned earlier, it vanishes.

8

Answering your doubts about contemplation;
why learning, curiosity, and intellect must
be destroyed; and the difference between the
active and contemplative life

But now you ask me: "How am I supposed to know if these thoughts are good or evil? And how can they be evil if they help me worship God? I'm completely baffled. Meditating on Christ's Passion or on my sinfulness comforts me. Such thoughts make me cry, and the godly sorrow has done me much good. How can that be evil? And if these thoughts are good, as I think they are, I'm amazed you want me to 'put them down' and abandon them under the cloud of forgetting."

You've asked excellent questions, and I'll try to answer them as best I can.[1] First, you want to know more about the thoughts that interrupt your contemplative time, incessantly offering help. This is just how your mind works. You're watching your soul reason. When you wonder, "Is this good or evil?" I have to say that obviously it's a good thing because your ability to reason is a reflection of God. However, you can use it for good or evil. The thoughts that help you understand, with grace, your own frailties, Christ's Passion, and God's amazing blessings, are good. I'm not surprised that they deepen your devotion. But when these very same meditations become infected with pride and when the educated ego starts believing in its own scholarly expertise, students fail to become humble scholars and masters of divinity and devotion, becoming arrogant scholars instead, masters of vanity and lies, aligned with the devil. This warning applies to everyone. Secular or religious, if your mind is inflated by pride or seduced by worldly pleasures, positions, and honors, or if you crave wealth, status, and the flattery of others, your God-given ability to reason is serving evil.

Next, you ask me why you should place these meditations under the cloud of forgetting. After all, they're good thoughts, and when well used, they nurture your devotional life. I answer by describing for you the two kinds of lives in the Church, the active and the contemplative. The active life is lower, the contemplative higher, and both have two stages, also a lower and a higher.[2] These two lives are complementary and so bound together that, although each is quite distinct, neither can exist without the other. The higher stage of the active life is also the lower stage of the contemplative life. That's why you can't be truly active unless you participate in the contemplative life, and you can't be fully contemplative unless you participate in the active life. The active life starts and ends on earth, but the contemplative life begins on earth and never ends. Mary chose this eternal path that can never be taken away.[3] Though the active life is anxious and there are always problems,[4] the contemplative life sits in peace, focused on one thing.

In the lower stage of the active life, you learn genuine acts of mercy and practice loving. In the higher stage of the active life (synonymous with the lower stage of contemplative living), your spirit becomes preoccupied with looking, and you start spending time in meditation. In this higher active stage (lower contemplative), your mind steeps in remorse for your flaws and mistakes, while you reflect on Christ's Passion and the ways his followers have suffered. Too, your amazement at God's mercy grows as you ponder his kindness and count your blessings, and you begin thanking God for his wonderful presence throughout creation. But the higher stage of contemplation, as far as we can know it here on earth, is only darkness[5] and the cloud of unknowing, and once we are in these, we find that loving nudges[6] lead us into a blind gazing at the naked being of God alone.

The lower stage of active life requires extroversion and takes place between you and the world under you, so to speak, while the higher stage of the active (lower stage of the contemplative) becomes interior, and you start getting acquainted with yourself. But in the higher stage of the contemplative life, your interactions take place above you, between you and God. In this way, you transcend yourself, achieving by grace what you can't do on your own—union with the God of love and freedom.

If you're going to advance to the higher stage of the active life, temporarily stop engaging in its lower stage, just as you must suspend practice of the lower stage of the contemplative life to advance to its higher stage. That's why when you meditate, you must not let your mind turn to your life and to things that you have done or are planning to do, even if these are good deeds. This approach will seem odd at first. That's also why when you advance in kindness to working in the darkness of the cloud of unknowing, you must not even let yourself be distracted by thoughts of God's blessings and goodness, even though they are holy thoughts that make you feel good.

So let go of every clever, persuasive thought. Put it down and cover it with a thick cloud of forgetting. No matter how sacred, no thought can ever promise to help you in the work of contemplative prayer, because only love—not knowledge—can help us reach God. As long as you are a soul living in a mortal body, your intellect, no matter how sharp and spiritually discerning, never sees God perfectly. The mind is always distorted in some way, warping our work; and at its worst, our intellect can lead us to great error.

*How even the holiest thoughts obstruct
rather than help contemplative work*

So then, you must suppress the sharp intrusions of your thoughts that inevitably come when you sit down to do the blind work of contemplation. You must defeat them, or they'll defeat you. Here's why. If you're not careful, you will think you're resting in this darkness, with nothing in your mind but God, until you look and see that your mind is actually not occupied in this darkness but is watching a clear picture of something associated with God, which is less than he is. When that happens, this attribute is above you and between you and your God. So, no matter how sacred or pleasant these lucid images are, let go of them.

Let me tell you something. For your soul to be healthy, it most needs a blind stirring of love for God alone. When your secret[1] love beats on the cloud of unknowing, it pleases God and the heavenly community more than anything else and benefits you and all of your friends and acquaintances, both living and dead. This purest loving feeling is also better for you than anything else. It's even better than having the eye of your soul opened during contemplation to a vision of the angels and saints, or your being allowed to hear the joyful singing of those living in heaven.

Don't be surprised. Once you experience the truth of my words, you'll understand. When grace helps you grasp this fact, you'll agree with me. You'll never see anything very clearly in this life, but you can certainly grope your way toward God. In love and longing, then, enter that cloud. What I mean is—let God's love draw you to him. His kindness will teach you how to forget everything else.

Consider this. If the simplest thought rises, unasked, in your mind, distracting you, taking you away from God in will and understanding and weakening your ability to taste the fruit of his love, how much more will you be stymied if you willingly cultivate thoughts during the work of contemplation? And if your contemplation of a particular saint or of any other purely spiritual topic presents obstacles to your work, how much worse will the interruption be if your mind dwells on someone you know or on some material possession or other worldly concern?

Having good, pure thoughts pop into your head spontaneously or deliberately is not evil. I never meant that. God forbid if anyone thought I did. No, I mean that these ideas, though wholly commendable, will get in the way of your praying contemplatively. They hurt more than they help during this work. When you are seeking God, you won't rest until you rest in him; the imperfect meditation on one of his saints or angels will not satisfy.

10

How to tell which thoughts are sinful,
and which are mortal or venial

Not every thought is alike, however.[1] Sometimes—out
of the blue—a naked thought of someone you know or
of something worldly will press on your will and understanding, and although this thought is no sin but is
merely the consequence of the original sin you inherited
and must deal with, and even though baptism has
cleansed you of its guilt, you are still responsible for
striking down these thoughts as quickly as they come.
If you don't, your weak human nature is likely to succumb to them, as your secular heart remembers the
good experiences and delights in their pleasure a second
time, or recalls the bad experiences and gives in to
resentment, complaining inside again.

For worldly men and women living in mortal sin,
entertaining such thoughts can be deadly. For you and
all others who have honestly renounced the world,
publicly or privately, to live devout lives, fastening your

secular heart on these thoughts is less serious, because you don't encourage them to stay. Long ago, you grounded and rooted your intent in God, choosing to be ruled not by your own will but by the wisdom of your mentors. But if you leave these thoughts alone there, you might as well be gluing them to your spiritual heart, which is your will, and then the attachment becomes a deadly sin.

For example, if you find yourself obsessing on someone, on some physical injury, or on some painful conversation, you risk becoming a bitter person obsessed with revenge, which is the sin of anger. If you let your soul feel total contempt and loathing for someone, and if you're always insulting and censuring them in your mind, you're living with envy. If you give in to a feeling of malaise and exhaustion, that's laziness. On the other hand, if you find yourself entertaining ideas so pleasant that you could rest in them forever, only to realize that these thoughts are all about your own natural goodness, accomplishments, intelligence, talents, position, or beauty, this is pride. And if you dwell on your wealth and what you own (or want to own), then that's greed. If you're preoccupied with lots and lots of food and drink and only the best will do, you know gluttony. And if you're seduced by an inordinate love of giving or receiving flattery and by a deep-seated need to be liked, or by sexual pleasures, this is lust.[2]

11

*How to evaluate each thought and impulse
and avoid being careless about venial sin*

I don't say these things to you because I believe that
you or any other person of prayer is guilty of such sins
or feels burdened by them. But I do want you to evaluate every thought you have. Develop an awareness of
how each one influences your behavior. If you catch a
tempting idea when it first arises, you can stop it from
leading you into sin. Work hard at mental vigilance.
And I have to warn you that, no matter who you are,
if you get careless about what you're thinking, even if
you've not yet sinned, eventually you'll be caught in
some sort of indiscretion. Stay alert. Your first line of
defense is paying attention to the sudden allure of each
thought. There's no way you can totally avoid missteps
in this life, but that doesn't mean you can relax your
guard, either. On the path of purity and spiritual
growth, you can't afford a reckless attitude toward even
the smallest sin. Such nonchalance can only lead to an
involvement with deadly sins.

12

*How contemplation destroys sin
and nurtures virtues*[1]

So if you want to stand and not fall into sin, never let go of your purpose and don't let anything take away your longing for God. With the sharp spear of your love, never stop beating on the cloud of unknowing that is between you and your God. Don't give up, for any reason, regardless of what happens. The work of contemplation is the only thing that destroys the foundation and the root of sin. For no matter how long you fast, how late you watch, how early you rise, how hard your bed, or how prickly your hair shirt, these disciplines help you very little. Even if you were allowed (and you're not!) to put out your eyes, cut out your tongue, plug up your ears and nose, cut off your private parts,[2] or in other ways inflict pain on your body, that wouldn't help you conquer your capacity for sin.

Plus, even if you grieved unendingly for your sins, spent copious amounts of time weeping over them or

Christ's Passion, or constantly reflected on the joys of heaven, what would you get? I admit that these are good. Yes, they help you grow in grace, but when compared to the blind stirring of love and its benefits, they seem puny indeed. Contemplative work is love at its best. Mary chose this "best part."[3] It trumps everything else and is complete on its own, while any meditations on sin, sorrow, the Passion, and heaven are nothing without it. Contemplative work not only pulls out sin's roots—it grows goodness in its place. All virtues are found in contemplation. Without it, people may have virtues, but they will always be shallow and twisted by self-interest.

Virtue is nothing more than a mature[4] and deliberate affection plainly directed at God, for him alone. He is the only reason goodness exists. He himself is the pure source of every virtue, and if anyone is motivated by anything other than God, even if God is their main goal, their virtue is suspect. We can prove this statement true by considering two of the virtues. Take a look at humility and unselfish love. If you have these, do you need any others? No, you've got everything then.

13

Humility, and when it is "perfect" and "imperfect"

Next, we'll look at the virtue of humility. If you want to develop "perfect" humility, you must understand that God alone is its source. Any other motive taints your humility, making it "imperfect," even if you are bent on serving God. As we explore the nature of humility, these differences will become clear.

Basically, humility is seeing yourself as you really are. It's that simple. Two truths make this obvious. We are sordid, sad, weak creatures. Everyone lives with these consequences of original sin, because no matter how much you advance in holiness, you can never be wholly free of them to some degree. But being aware of your imperfections is humility of the "imperfect" sort. "Perfect" humility comes when you experience God's goodness and superabundant love. Nature trembles before God's majesty and kindness, scholars are reduced to fools, and saints and angels go blind. Words fail me[1] when I think what would happen to us all if

God in his wisdom didn't measure out the revelation of himself to match our ability and the progress of grace in our lives.

Humility gained from an experiential knowledge of God's love is the only "perfect" kind, because you'll know it forever, even in eternity. On the other hand, an understanding of our human failings is considered "imperfect" humility because it's temporary in two ways. When we die, it vanishes. Also, sometimes it will stop working before then, when abundant grace creates a very brief moment of ecstasy for the person steeped in contemplative work. God can suddenly allow that soul in a mortal body to feel completely taken out of itself, where all understanding and awareness of being vanish, and in this state of forgetfulness, the person is no longer concerned with categories like *holy* and *sinful*.

For some, this ecstasy happens often; for others, rarely. Either way, it never lasts long, but during that brief moment the person is absolutely humble, knowing and feeling God alone. So remember that being conscious of your shortcomings is not the same as "perfect" humility. I'm not, however, suggesting that you ignore your weaknesses—not at all. Don't misunderstand me. I believe self-awareness is a constant necessity and will always be beneficial to us here on earth.

14

---

*Why we must go through imperfect humility to
reach perfect humility—because we're sinful*

Even though I call self-knowledge an "imperfect" humility, I value it highly. Because even if every saint, angel
in heaven, and church member (at every level of maturity, religious or lay) did nothing but constantly petition God on my behalf, asking that I grow in humility,
their prayers would not help me achieve this growth as
much as if I possess a real understanding of who I am.
Self-knowledge is the only way to get and keep the
virtue of humility.

Don't flinch in the face of the tremendous work
involved. Get to know yourself. Yes, it is backbreaking
labor. Embrace it. Through it, you'll experience God
as he is. I don't mean you'll know God completely.
That's not possible for anyone on earth. Nor do I mean
you'll know him as you will in the absolute joy of eternity, when body and soul are truly one. But when you
get to know yourself better as the mortal human you

are, your soul grows in humility, and you'll know God as fully as possible on earth.

Don't think for a minute that because I described two kinds of humility, calling one "perfect" and the other "imperfect," that I mean for you to stop working at the "imperfect" and focus wholly on the "perfect." I trust you'll never do that, because if you neglect the work of the first, never rising to the challenge of getting to know yourself, you can't mature in humility. It just won't happen.

My purpose in discussing this subject with you is that, first, I want you to appreciate the singular worth of contemplative work. This spiritual discipline is better than any other. Here's why. Through it, you become acquainted with perfect humility, when, by grace, you allow the hidden love of your pure heart to press against the dark cloud of unknowing between you and God. This impulse is perfect humility. It occurs without any special images or clear ideas. I also want you to be able to recognize perfect humility so you can set it up in your heart as a sign of love. It becomes something to aim for. Do this for you and for me. I believe that the mere awareness of perfect humility will help you be more humble.

We've discussed humility because I've noticed that ignorance often triggers pride. I was worried that if you did not understand humility's two stages, you might confuse imperfect humility with the perfect kind. A little self-knowledge is not the ultimate goal. Don't deceive yourself. Perfect humility is not a destination. Those who believe that they've "arrived" have merely found another way to wrap themselves up in filthy, stinking pride. So, set your heart on working toward perfect humility. The person who experiences it won't want to sin, not then, nor for a long time after.

15

---

*An argument against the claim that perfect
humility is being mindful of your own sinfulness*

Believe me when I say that perfect humility does exist
and that grace can help you experience it in this life. I
want to prove that those who believe otherwise are
wrong. Some say that the best way to perfect humility
is by meditating on our weaknesses and on the sins we
have committed in the past.[1] I want to refute this error.

I will admit that those who sin on a regular basis (and
I have and do) need this sort of self-reflection. We must
be humbled by the memory of our sinfulness and past
mistakes, until the awful rust of sin is scrubbed away
in an awesome manner,[2] as witnessed by our conscience
and spiritual director.

But there is another, better way that's best for all
concerned. Some who want to be contemplatives are
comparatively innocent. They don't know what it's
like to sin dangerously and on purpose. Having never

chosen immorality deliberately, fully aware of the consequences, they've only fallen through human frailty and ignorance. On the other hand, we who have known serious sin can choose purification through forgiveness, and our spiritual directors and consciences witness our remorse, confession, and penance in the Holy Church; then we, too, can feel stirred and called by grace to be contemplatives. For both of us, the best way to grow in humility is not through reflecting on our weaknesses but by remembering God's goodness and love. This second way is as far above self-knowledge as the life of our Lady St. Mary is superior to that of the most sinful penitent in the Holy Church or as the life of Christ is superior to the life of any person on earth or as a heavenly angel who has never known and will never know imperfection is superior to the weakest person in this world.

If we had no other reason for humility than that of being aware of and feeling bad about our imperfections, how could those who never sinned and never even felt the temptation to sin be humble? This was the case with our Lord Jesus Christ, our Lady St. Mary, and every saint and angel in heaven. In the Gospel, our Lord calls us to seek the perfection of purity, a maturity that requires us to develop humility and every other virtue.[3] He led this life inherently, and we can live this life through grace.

16

How the sinner, converted and called to contemplation, experiences perfection sooner than through any other work, immediately receiving God's forgiveness of sin

---

Know this. True repentance is never considered presumptuous. Anyone can repent. Even the worst sinners alive may offer God this humble impulse of love, secretly pressing against that cloud of unknowing between them and God. The only requirements are the desire for contemplation, the consent of a spiritual mentor, and approval from your conscience. Mary Magdalene represents all sinners called to the contemplative life, and our Lord said to her, "Your sins are forgiven."[1] Did he forgive her because her godly sorrow was profound or because she was mindful of her sins or because she had reflected on her weaknesses until she was humbled? Why did he tell her, "Your sins are forgiven"? Because she loved much—amazing! Look how powerful this secret nudge of love is. It gets the Lord's attention. It's stronger than anything.

I completely agree that Mary Magdalene was also filled with godly sorrow. She wept painfully for her sins, and in being mindful of them, was humbled. We must do the same. Those of us who have been awful, chronic sinners all our lives must embrace a cataclysmic, life-altering sorrow and regret. We must know what it's like to be humbled, aware of our sinfulness.

But how? Do as Mary did. Her way is best. She could not stop feeling a deep, heartfelt regret for her sins, for this pain accompanied her wherever she went, a burden wrapped up and secretly hidden in the hole of her heart, but not forgotten;[2] and yet we see in Scripture that she had an even more heartfelt[3] sorrow and a sadder[4] longing and a deeper sigh and a greater despair—even almost to the point of death—for the inadequacy of her love, though she had a great love. Don't let this surprise you. It's simply the nature of true lovers. The more they love, the more they long to love.

She knew she was the worst sinner of all. Deep down, she knew this saddest truth. She also knew that her sins were a gulf separating her from the God she loved so much, and she understood that they made her feel terribly sick for failing in love. So what did she do? Did she come down from the heights of her loving desire into the depths of her sinful life, so that she could search there in the polluted, stinking swamp and dunghill[5] of her sins, scrutinizing each one up and down, analyzing every circumstance, and weeping over each one separately? No, she didn't do that at all. Why not? God taught her deep within her soul, by his grace, that this approach would be futile. But if she had tried this way, she would probably have revived in herself a willingness to sin, rather than gaining full forgiveness of her sins.

So Mary hung up[6] her love and longing in this cloud of unknowing and learned to love what she could never clearly see with her mind nor feel with her emotions. Sometimes she became so immersed in this sweetness that she had little real awareness of herself as a sinner. It's true! In fact, I expect that because Mary deeply loved her Lord's divinity, she hardly noticed his beautiful human self. She didn't have eyes for his sacred, blessed, gorgeous body, or for the way he moved when he sat and spoke with her. In fact, the Gospel suggests that when he taught her, she became oblivious to everything in this world.[7]

———

*How true contemplatives forget the active
life, ignoring negative things done to or
spoken about them and making no attempt
to justify themselves to their critics*

———

In the Gospel of St. Luke, we read about our Lord's
visit to the house of Martha, Mary's sister. While he
was there, Martha bustled about, preparing his food
and drink, while Mary merely sat at his feet.[1] Mary was
so absorbed in listening to his teaching that she paid no
attention whatsoever to her sister Martha's busy service. Helpful, holy service is the first stage of the active
life. Mary also paid no attention to the beauty of the
Lord's sacred body or his pleasing human voice and
conversation, though that would have been better and
holier than busy service, since it is the second stage of
the active life (and the first stage of the contemplative).
No, Mary focused instead on the highest wisdom of his
divinity concealed in the enigmatic teaching of his humanity. She paid complete attention to him in this way,

with every ounce of love in her heart, not moving a muscle, disregarding anything said about her and anything going on around her. And her delightful, intimate love pressed against that high cloud of unknowing between her and God.

I have to tell you that there's never been and never will be anyone who doesn't have this high and wonderful cloud of unknowing between them and God, no matter how pure they are and no matter the heights of ecstasy they experience while contemplating and loving the divine Being.[2] In this cloud, Mary was busy with the private yearnings of her love. Why? This is the best, holiest part of contemplation, and Mary wouldn't leave it for any reason. Even when Martha complained, asking the Lord to tell her sister Mary to get up and help her so she wouldn't have to do all of the work by herself, Mary sat still, answering not a word, not even frowning. No wonder—she had other work to do that Martha couldn't see. Mary had no leisure time to listen to her sister or to answer her criticism.[3]

Do you see, my friend? The actions, words, and looks shared between our Lord and these two sisters teach a lesson to all active and contemplative persons of the Church, from then until the day of judgment. Mary represents all contemplatives, who should model their lives on hers, and in the same way Martha represents all actives, who do well to follow her life as a guide.

18

That still, to this day, actives complain
about contemplatives, out of ignorance,
just as Martha complained about Mary

Just as Martha criticized Mary, to this day, active persons complain about contemplatives. Whenever anyone belonging to any religious or secular group in this world feels the stirring through grace and good advice to relinquish all worldly business and embrace the contemplative life as best they can following their conscience and the advice of a wise spiritual director, without exception, their brothers, sisters, closest friends, and many others who don't understand their reasons or the life of contemplation start complaining loudly all at once, sharply opposing this decision and belittling it as a waste of time.[1] As fast as they can, these people dig up many untrue stories, as well as many true ones, of men and women who have chosen this path and lapsed into sin; they never tell the story of the person who became a contemplative and stood strong.

Yes, many of those who seemed to have renounced the world for the contemplative life have transgressed—I grant that. It does happen. Because they would not submit to and be ruled by authentic spiritual counsel, they did not become God's servants and his contemplatives, but the devil's. They became hypocrites or heretics and fell into madness and immorality, slandering the Holy Church with scandals. But I'll stop here, before taking us too far off course. Later perhaps, if God allows and we need to, I might say more about these people and why they failed. But we'll leave them now and continue with our subject.

19

---

*The author's brief apology, teaching contemplatives
to excuse actives for
complaining and acting against them*

Some may think I have shown too little respect for Martha, that special saint, by comparing her complaints about Mary with those made by worldly people criticizing contemplatives. Actually, I mean no disrespect to her or to them. God forbid that I should say anything derogatory in this book about any of God's servants, whatever their stage of holiness, let alone about his special friend, Martha. In fact, we should excuse Martha for complaining. We must take into consideration the circumstances and how she spoke. She said what she said from ignorance; she simply didn't know what Mary was doing.

This shouldn't surprise us. I doubt Martha had ever heard of the soul's purification through such contemplation, so she couldn't understand that Mary was busy, too, but in a different way. Plus, Martha was polite and kept her criticism brief, so we should exonerate her fully.

In the same way and for the same reasons, I believe that we should overlook worldly men and women whose ignorance leads them to criticize contemplatives, though sometimes they are rude in the way they word their disapproval. They only understand the active life, just as Martha understood little to nothing about Mary's contemplative work. The same thing happens today. People are baffled when God's young disciples withdraw from this world's activities to be God's special friends in purity and kindness of spirit. I believe that if others did understand contemplative prayer, they would never condemn or oppose it. That's why I think detractors should always be forgiven. They only know one way of living, their own active path, and can imagine nothing better.

We should also forgive them because we ourselves are not entirely free of ignorance. When I consider the countless mistakes I've made out of not knowing something, I realize that for God to forgive me for these, I must find the love and compassion within me to forgive others of the same blunders. Otherwise, I'm certainly not treating them the way I wish they'd treat me.

20

How the all-powerful God well defends those who won't stop loving him through contemplative prayer to stick up for themselves

That's why I think anyone committed to the contemplative life should not only pardon actives for finding fault with them, but should also be so engrossed in their spiritual work that they hardly even notice what anyone else says about or does to them. Follow Mary Magdalene, our very best example. If we do, our Lord will do for us now what he did for Mary then.[1]

And what was that? Definitely this. Christ responded positively when Martha complained about her sister. When Martha demanded that our loving, omniscient Lord Jesus sit in judgment on Mary, he didn't. He could have turned right around and demanded that she get up and help Martha serve him, but he did better than that. He saw that Mary was so absorbed in loving him and contemplating his divinity that she wouldn't stop even to defend herself, so in his usual gentle manner, he answered for her, reasoning with Martha. He became Mary's advocate and defended her for loving him.

What did he say? He called out, "Martha, Martha!" He said it twice, to be sure she heard him. He wanted her to pay close attention to what he had to say. "You are worried,"[2] he continued, "and distracted by many things." Here he means that actives are always busy, preoccupied with a long, diverse to-do list, first meeting their own needs and keeping their lives running smoothly, and then doing kind, merciful deeds to their neighbors,[3] as love requires. He wanted Martha to realize that her good works[4] contributed to her spiritual health, but he didn't want her to think that it was the best work of all, so he added, "There is need of only one thing."

And what do you think that one thing is? Surely he means we must love and praise God alone, for his own sake, before any other physical or spiritual activity. There's nothing more important. He wanted Martha to know that. He didn't want her to think that she could love and praise God above all concerns *and* also be busy with the affairs of this life. He wanted her to see that she could never perfectly serve God physically and spiritually; everyday concerns and contemplation are always an imperfect mix. So he added, "Mary has chosen the best part, which will not be taken away from her." He told her "it will not be taken away" because the work of perfect love, the pure reaching out to God that begins here on earth, is exactly the same love that will last eternally in the joy of heaven. It is all one love.

21

The true interpretation of the Gospel text,
"Mary has chosen the best part"

What is the meaning of "Mary has chosen the best part"? When we speak of "the best," we imply a good and a better. There must be at least three options for something to qualify as "the best," because it is the superlative degree. What were the three good choices from which Mary chose the best? She wasn't picking between three ways of life, because the Holy Church only speaks of two—the active and the contemplative. In this Gospel story these two ways of life are allegorically represented by the two sisters, Martha and Mary. Martha represents the active life, Mary the contemplative. Outside of these two lives, nobody can be saved, and when you're only given two choices, neither can be called "the best."

Although there are only two lives, active and contemplative, between them there are three parts, each one better than the last. We have already discussed these ascending stages in great detail, but I will go over them again briefly here. The first stage of the active life is made up of genuine good works of mercy and love, done physically. In the second stage, a person begins meditating in a good way on the deep truths of our sinfulness, Christ's Passion, and heaven's joy. The first stage is good, but the second stage is better because it is both the second part of the first life (the active) and the first part of the second life (the contemplative). These two stages overlap. They show the close spiritual relationship between the active and the contemplative lives, making them sisters like Martha and Mary. An active person may only advance this far in contemplation, except on rare occasions, and only then through a special grace. Conversely, on rare occasions and when greatly needed, a contemplative may return to this shared stage, but must not drop lower.

The third stage of these two lives hangs[1] in this dark cloud of unknowing, where we secretly launch many loving desires to God alone, to get to know him as he is, for his own sake. So, while the first stage is good and the second stage is better, the third stage is the best in every way. This is the "best part" Mary chose. You can clearly see now why our Lord didn't say, "Mary has chosen the best life," because there are only two lives to choose from, and from two alternatives, you can never select a "best." Instead, he said that from these two lifestyles, "Mary has chosen the best part, which will not be taken away from her."

Again, he said this because the first two stages, though good and purifying, end when we die. They stop when this life stops, because in the other, eternal life, there will be no need for works of mercy and no need to mourn our sinfulness and no need to grieve the Passion of Christ, since, unlike now, no one will be hungry, thirsty, deathly cold, sick, homeless, imprisoned, or needing burial, for no one will die then. If you feel grace is calling you to choose the third part, choose it with Mary. Let me clarify that. If God is calling you to the third part, lean on him and work hard, because it will never be taken away from you. If you begin it here, it will last forever.

So let the voice of our Lord call out to these actives, speaking on our behalf, as he did for Mary. "Martha, Martha!" he said then and even now he's saying, "Actives, actives! Work as hard as you can in the first and second stages, first one and then the other, or, if you feel like it and have the energy, be bold and do both simultaneously. Don't bother[2] contemplatives. You don't know what crosses they bear. Leave them alone. Let them sit in the peace of Mary's third and 'best' part, and play."[3]

22

Christ's wonderful love for Mary, who represents all sinners truly converted and called to the grace of contemplation

---

The love our Lord and Mary Magdalene had for each other was sweet. She loved him so much, and he loved her much more. If you could've seen the looks that passed between them, you'd know. This isn't gossip; it's the Gospel. Its witness is never anything but true. Read this story, and you'll see that their relationship was not superficial. Mary loved him completely, without holding back anything. In return, nothing less than Jesus satisfied her. This is the same Mary who looked for him at the sepulchre. She was weeping, and not even angels could comfort her, not even when they spoke to her gently and lovingly, saying, "Don't cry, Mary, for our Lord whom you seek is risen, and you'll see him again among his disciples in Galilee, as he promised. You'll have him, alive again, in all his beauty."[1] This assurance didn't stop her tears. She wasn't looking for angels, but for their King.

What else? Surely anyone who studies[2] this Gospel story will find many wonderful examples of Mary's perfect love. They seem specifically written to instruct contemplatives. They do in fact serve that purpose for those who are discerning. If you look at our Lord's amazing personal love for Mary and recognize in it the love he has for all of us ordinary sinners who genuinely repent and are called by grace to the contemplative life, then you'll see why our Lord won't allow anyone, man or woman, not even Mary's own sister, to speak a word against her, without defending her himself. And there's one more thing! He even told off Simon the Leper in his own house. Why? For thinking harshly of Mary. This was an intense, exceptional love.[3]

23

---

*How God answers and provides spiritually for
those who are too preoccupied with loving him
to answer and provide for themselves*

I promise you this: if we pattern our love and way of
living on Mary Magdalene's as best we can through grace
and wise counsel, God will always defend us as he defended her. Every day he'll secretly speak to the hearts
of anyone who criticizes us, aloud or in their thoughts.
I'm not saying that we will ever be without critics. Detractors are a given, as they were for Mary. I am saying
that we should take just as much notice of what they say
and think as she did—we shouldn't let it disrupt our
interior, spiritual work, because she didn't. Our Lord
will answer them, and, if they are good-hearted, they
will hear him and before long, they will feel ashamed
when they remember their critical words and thoughts.

He not only answers for us and defends us spiritually, he also moves in others' spirits, making them want
to give us life's necessities, such as food, clothes, and

all else, when he sees that we won't abandon the work of loving him to busy ourselves procuring these. I say this to refute the error of those who claim that you can't start living the contemplative life until you first make sure you've provided for all of your material needs. They're fond of saying that God sends the cow, but not by the horn.[1] But they slander God and know it. Trust God's faithfulness. When you truly turn your back on the world to serve him, he will never disappoint you, whoever you are. God always provides one of two things (without your help): either an abundance of what you need or the physical stamina and spiritual patience to endure its absence. What does it matter what we have? It's all one to the true contemplative.

Those doubting this truth—and it doesn't matter who they are—have either let the devil in to rob their hearts of faith, or else, no matter how wise and holy they talk, they have not yet committed their lives to God as they should.

So, if you commit yourself to being a true contemplative as Mary was, choose to be humbled by the amazing glory and goodness of God, who is perfect, rather than by your own sinfulness, which is imperfect. In other words, focus on God's excellence, rather than on your inferiority. Those who are perfectly humble lack nothing, physically or spiritually, because God is all abundance. Yes, those who have him—as this book explains—need nothing else in this life.

24

---

*What love is, and how it is mysteriously
and perfectly contained in the
contemplative work of this book*

Without a doubt, humility and charity and every other
fruit of the spirit fill this little, blind love tap beating
against that dark cloud of unknowing, and all things are
patted down, and all cares forgotten.[1] For charity is
nothing more than loving God for himself above every
creature and also loving your neighbor as you do yourself, for God's sake. Obviously, contemplative work
requires that we love God simply for being God, more
than anything else.

As mentioned earlier, the essence of this work is
nothing but a naked intent, a simple reaching out to
God for himself. I call this a "naked intent" because it
requires total detachment. The student apprenticed to
perfection doesn't ask to be released from suffering or
to get a bigger reward. No, to put it briefly, the disciple of contemplative prayer only wants to know God

better. Contemplatives ignore their own suffering or happiness, because they only want the will of the One they love to be fulfilled. It's obvious, then, that God is perfectly loved for himself alone in this work, because the experienced contemplative won't allow thoughts of even the holiest creature made by God to intrude on their prayers.

Experience shows that the work of contemplation completely satisfies the requirements of the second, lower command of charity, which is "love your neighbor." While engaged in this work, the mature contemplative has no special relationship with anyone in particular, whether family or stranger, friend or enemy, because everyone is family and no one is a stranger, and everyone is friend and no one is an enemy. The genuine lover of God takes this love even further. Those who cause contemplatives pain or stress are considered their very special friends, and contemplatives wish them every good thing, just as they do their closest friend.

25

*That the perfect soul never thinks about anyone
in particular during contemplative prayer*

I'm saying that during contemplation, don't have any
special relationships. Forget everyone, friend or enemy,
family or stranger. To do this work perfectly, you must
neglect everything that is not God. And let me tell you
what this discipline will do for you. It will change your
heart. It will make you so kind and dynamic in loving
that when you stop doing it and mingle with the world
again, coming down from contemplation to converse
with or pray for your neighbor, you'll discover that you
love your slanderer as much as your friend, and that you
love any stranger as much as a relative—in fact, sometimes you'll be more partial to your enemy than to your
friend. I'm not saying that you should ever completely
abandon the work of contemplation, which would be a
sin, but you will find that the demands of love sometimes
require you to shift gears out of contemplative prayer,
so that you can care for others.

In the work of contemplation, however, there's no time for analyzing people into the categories of friend or enemy, relative or stranger. Yes, of course you'll continue to feel closer to some than to others. It's only natural, and there's nothing wrong with that. Love has its reasons. Look at Christ. He felt a deeper affection for John, Mary, and Peter than for all others. That's fine, but what I'm saying is that during the work of contemplation, you should feel the same intimate love for everyone, because your only reason to love is God. Plain and simple, all people must be loved for God, and they must be loved just as well as you love yourself.

We all strayed when Adam did, and our good works prove that we want to be and can be saved through Christ's death. The soul perfectly committed to the work of contemplation becomes one with God in spirit and loves sacrificially, as Christ did. You wish wholeness on everyone you know. Remember how your body reacts when your arm aches? The pain radiates, making you hurt all over in sympathy. But if your arm is fine, your whole body rejoices. The same is true with the spiritual arms and legs of the Church. Christ is our head, and we are his limbs, if we live and move in love.[1]

If we want to be mature disciples of our Lord, we must strain every spiritual muscle learning to love our neighbors, who are our brothers and sisters. For their salvation we must be willing to sacrifice all, as Christ did on the Cross. How did he do this? Our Lord did not play favorites. He didn't sacrifice himself only for his family, his friends, and the ones who loved him best, his closest friends. He offered himself to all humanity, for anyone who abandons sin and asks for mercy will be saved through the power of his Passion.

As I said before, this little act of loving called contemplation mysteriously contains humility and charity, as well as all the other virtues.

26

_____

That without special grace or a long commitment to ordinary grace, contemplative work is very hard, and how the soul absolutely requires grace for this work, while grace, in turn, is God's work alone

_____

So work hard for a while and beat on this high cloud of unknowing; then rest. As you do it, don't be surprised how difficult it is—yes, you'll have a hard time, unless you receive special grace or have done it for so long that it has become a habit.

Let's step back a minute and look at contemplation. Why does it have to be so hard? After all, that profound love stirring again and again in your will requires no straining on your part. These gentle impulses don't come from you but from the hand of God, the all-powerful, always ready to start this work in anyone who's done everything possible to get prepared. Then what makes this work so difficult? I'll tell you. You must tread down thoughts of every creature that God has ever made and then hold them there, keeping them covered under the cloud of forgetting we discussed earlier. This is the hard work. God's grace will help you roll your sleeves up for it, but you still have to do it yourself. On the other hand, God alone sets those loving feelings in motion. So do your part, and I can promise you God will do his. He never fails.

Get on with it then. Be faithful. Work hard. I'm watching to see how well you do. Can't you see him standing there, waiting for you? Shame on you for doubting! Work conscientiously for a stretch and soon you'll feel the enormity and difficulties of this work ease. Yes, in the beginning it seems demanding and severe, when you're not yet used to it, but as your devotion grows, contemplation ceases being hard and instead becomes very restful and easy. It will hardly seem like work. God will sometimes do it for you then, all by himself, but not every time and never for long; only when he feels like it and in the way he feels like doing it. When that happens, you'll be happy to leave him alone to do as he wants.

Sometimes God may send out a ray of divine light, piercing this cloud of unknowing between you and him and letting you see some of his ineffable mysteries. You'll feel on fire with his love then. I can't describe this experience. It's beyond words. My foolish, human tongue can't describe God's grace. Even if I dared, I would refuse, and that's that. But I'm happy to talk with you about your part in contemplation and how you should respond when you feel stirred and helped[1] by grace, because it's less dangerous to discuss your role.

27

Who should engage in this work of grace

First and foremost, I want to tell you who should take up contemplative work and when and how and what discernment you'll need in it. If you ask me who should do this work, here's my answer: everyone who genuinely forsakes the world and the active life to dedicate themselves to the contemplative life, whoever they are, whether or not they have ever been chronic sinners, should do this work of grace.

28

*How the persons who want to begin
contemplation must first thoroughly cleanse
their conscience of each sinful action,
as taught by the Church*

If you ask me when a person should begin contemplation, my answer is: you must have a clean conscience to begin. Consider each individual sin you've committed and repent, confess, atone, and determine to do better next time, as required by the Church.

No matter how well you confess sin and work to repair the harm done, the root and ground of transgression always remain in your soul, but the work of contemplation dries them up. Love heals. So if you want to do this work, cleanse your conscience first. Let yourself feel remorse. Confess and make amends, as the Church teaches. Then commit yourself to contemplative prayer boldly, humbly aware that you've been preparing a long time for it. Contemplative prayer is work of a lifetime, even if a person has never sinned in the worst of ways.

As long as I am a soul living in a mortal body, I will always see and feel this heavy cloud of unknowing between me and God. So will you. It's also true that because of the pain of original sin, we forever fight distraction, always contending with thoughts of others and situations wedging themselves between us and God. Here's why. God in his wisdom and judgment gave humans sovereignty and stewardship over all creatures, but that authority was lost when the human bowed to the proposal of subordinates, disobeying the Creator. That's why when we want to please God now, we always feel that the creatures that should be beneath us and under our control, press obstinately down on us from above, between us and our God.[1]

29

---

*That you must practice contemplative prayer
patiently; persist, endure its pain,
and judge no one*

So, if you want to recover the purity you had but lost
to sin, and if you wish to gain a well-being pain can't
puncture, choose this path. Do the work patiently. Accept its pain, whoever you are, whether you've led a
life of sin or not.

It's hard for everyone. Both sinners and those innocent of huge sins find it tough going, but it's much
harder for the person accustomed to sinning, which
only makes sense.

However, don't be surprised if sometimes those we
consider the "worst" sinners—I mean people who've
done horrible things—advance more quickly in this
work than those we regard as relatively "innocent."
These are merciful miracles of our Lord. God is generous with his grace, and the world looks on, astonished.
I sincerely believe that Judgment Day will be bright,

because we'll clearly see God and all of his gifts. On that day of ultimate truth, many of the "nobodies" of this world, now despised and neglected as lowlifes and hardened sinners, will claim their right to sit beside God's saints in God's sight. On the other hand, some who now seem so holy, and who are honored as if they were angels, and who perhaps never did commit a deadly sin, may find themselves sitting beside hell's devils in complete misery.

My point is—don't judge. No person on earth should be judged by another. Nobody can say whether what someone else does is "good" or "evil." That said, yes, you can scrutinize a person's actions, weigh them in your mind, and determine whether the deeds themselves are good or evil, but you cannot judge the person.

30

*Who can criticize and counsel
others about their faults*

So—I ask you—who can judge another's actions? Those invested with the authority to care for others' souls, and this authority can be granted publicly by the command and ordination of the Holy Church or privately by the Holy Spirit, who may inspire a person to shoulder this responsibility in a loving, mature way. We all need a reminder here, however. Never casually assume that you're meant to take on this power. Don't rush to judge anyone's mistakes and don't be a fault-finder. Only speak out if you feel the nudge of the Holy Spirit during contemplative prayer. Those who arrogate this responsibility to themselves find it's terribly easy for things to go wrong. So beware of that. Judge yourself as you want—that's between you and God or your spiritual director—but leave others alone.

31

*How the beginner in contemplation must
deal with thoughts and sinful impulses*

Once you feel you've done your best to amend your life
according to the ways and judgment of the Church, get
to work. Embrace the discipline of contemplative prayer
in earnest. At first, you may find certain memories keep
pushing on your mind between you and God, or you may
feel new temptations stirring in you. If so, be brave. Rise
above each one and depend on love's energy to help you
stamp them down under your feet. Try covering them
with a thick cloud of forgetting, as if they had never been
done by you or by anyone else. Forget them. If they
return again and again, reject them again and again. In
short, when they come up, put them down. If this work
becomes too hard, you'll need to develop a few spiritual
tricks and feints and secret stratagems[1] to help you deal
with your incessant thoughts. Such wisdom is best
learned from God through the experience of contemplative prayer than from any human teacher.

32

*Two spiritual tactics that help the
beginner in prayer*

In spite of what I said earlier, I'll tell you some of what
I know about these spiritual strategies for dealing with
incessant thoughts. Try them out and improve on them,
if you can do better.

When distracting thoughts press down on you, when
they stand between you and God and stubbornly de-
mand your attention, pretend you don't even notice
them. Try looking over their shoulders, as if you're
searching for something else, and you are. That something else is God, hidden in a cloud of unknowing. Do
this, and I know the work of contemplation will start
getting easier for you. When tried and understood, this
spiritual technique is nothing but an intense longing for
God, the desire to feel and see him as we can here. This
longing is true love, and love always deserves the peace
it wins.

There's another trick you can try, if you want. When exhausted from fighting your thoughts, when you're unable to put them down, fall down before them and cower like a captive or a coward overcome in battle. Give up. Accept that it's foolish for you to fight them any longer. Do this, and you'll find that in the hands of your enemies, you are surrendering to God. Let yourself feel defeated. Accept your failure. And always keep this plan in mind because when you try it, you'll discover that you melt like water. You become supple. I also believe that when this attitude is genuine, it's nothing but seeing who you really are, a filthy wretch, worse than nothing.[1] This is humility.

The good news is that humility gets God's attention. He'll descend to avenge you against your enemies. Swooping in, he will snatch you up and then gently dry your spiritual eyes, the way a father saves his small child, who was standing at the point of death, facing snarling wild boars or raging, biting bears.

33

---

*How contemplative prayer purifies the soul of
individual sins and their lingering pain,
but there is still no such thing as perfect
rest in this life*

There are other strategies, but I won't go into them
right now, because when, by grace, you try these two
and prove their worth, I believe that you'll have more
to teach me then than I could ever teach you. I say that
because, although everything I've said about these
spiritual techniques is true, I myself am far from having
mastered them. So I ask you—help me by being diligent
in these contemplative stratagems, because the more
you learn, the more you can teach me.

Keep on trying. Work hard and stick with it. I'm
asking you to do this. Humbly accept the pain if the
going gets tough and nothing happens quickly. Look on
this work as your purgatory. Later, when the initial
rough patch is over and your pain subsides, you'll sense
that God has become your teacher and that by his grace

these contemplative techniques have become second nature to you and at that point I have no doubt you will be cleansed, not only of your sin but also of its pain. When I say "pain" here, I'm referring to the suffering that you have caused yourself, not the pain of original sin. The agony of original sin is something we must live with our whole lives, no matter how hard we work, but it's nothing compared to the more terrible pain of our personal sins. Still, accept that you will always have to work hard, because every day you will encounter fresh temptations springing up from original sin, and you are responsible for beating them back with the awesome, sharp, double-edged sword of discernment. Through such experiences, you learn that this life offers no real security and no lasting rest.

But don't turn back and don't give up and don't give in to a fear of failing. If you're given the grace to destroy the pain of your past sins, through ways we've just discussed or, even better, through ways you discover yourself, I'm certain the painful consequences of original sin and any new temptations you meet will hardly bother you at all.

34

---

*That God gives the grace for contemplation
freely and directly and that it can't be
achieved by any methods*

If you ask me how to actually contemplate, I have to
ask God in his immense grace and kindness to teach you
himself, because I'll admit that I can't tell you myself.
That shouldn't surprise you, because contemplation is
God's work. He chooses which souls participate, and
his decision isn't based on individual merit. Without
God's intervention, no saint or angel would even think
to desire contemplative love. I also believe our Lord
deliberately chooses lifelong sinners to do this work,
perhaps even more often than he selects others who
have not grieved him as much. He wants us to see that
he is all merciful and all powerful and can work however, wherever, and whenever he wants.

God does not give his grace to nor work his work
in someone incapable of receiving it. And nobody who

lacks this grace can get it on their own, for it's the gift of love, whether you are a sinner or not. God doesn't offer it as a reward for not sinning, and he doesn't withhold it from the habitual sinner. Notice I said "withhold" and not "withdraw." Guard against error here. Remember—the nearer we get to truth, the more responsibility we have to avoid error. What I'm saying is true, and I hope it makes sense. If it doesn't, put it down a while until God himself teaches you about it. Do as I say, and you won't strain yourself.

Beware of pride. It blasphemes God in his gifts and makes sinners bold. The truly humble will understand what I'm trying to say. Contemplative prayer is a gift, no strings attached. God gives it to anyone he wants. You can't earn it. The presence of this gift gives your soul the ability to possess it and feel it. In other words, if you've been given the blessing of contemplative prayer, you've also been given an aptitude for it. The aptitude doesn't exist without the gift itself. An aptitude for this work is synonymous with the work itself. Longing to pray is praying, and without that the soul is dead. You'll have as much of contemplative prayer as you will or desire, no more and no less, and yet it's not a will or a desire, but something ineffable that stirs your longing for something unknowable. It's best not to care if you ever know more than this or not. Just keep doing this work, more and more. I ask this of you— always be doing.

In short, let God's grace do with you what it wants. Let it lead you wherever it wishes. Let it work and you receive. Look on it, watch it, and leave it alone. Don't meddle with it, trying to help, as if you could assist grace. Fear that your interference could wreck everything. Instead, be the tree, and let it be the carpenter. Be the house, and let it be the homeowner living there. Become blind during contemplative prayer and cut yourself off from needing to know things. Knowledge hinders, not helps you in contemplation. Be content feeling moved in a delightful, loving way by something mysterious and unknown, leaving you focused entirely on God, with no other thought than of him alone. Let your naked desire rest there.

If this happens, know that God is the one who stirs your will and longing, all by himself, with no middleman. Nor does he need your help to do this. Don't be afraid of the devil, either; he can't come near you. No matter how clever the devil is, he can't violate your will, though sometimes he may try by indirect means. Not even a good angel can directly influence your will. In short, only God can touch you there.

My words have outlined what only experience can teach you clearly, that we come to contemplation directly, not through certain techniques. They can't make it happen. All good methods depend on contemplative prayer, while it depends on nothing. No routine leads to love.

35

*Three skills every contemplative beginner must
practice: reading, reflecting, and praying*

The contemplative beginner must, however, engage in certain exercises. These are the lesson, the meditation, and the orison, better known as reading, reflecting, and praying. You can learn more about these three activities in another book, where the author explains them better than I can, so I won't go into great detail here.[1] I will tell you this, though. Except for experienced contemplatives (what few of them we have), all beginners and those advancing in contemplation find these three exercises so interdependent as to seem inseparable. You must first read or hear a book read before you can reflect on it. Reading a book yourself and listening to its being read are the same activity, really. Theology students learn from reading books, and the congregation then "reads" the clergy when they preach the word of God. Contemplative beginners and intermediates must also steep their souls in reflection before true prayer can happen. Test this and see as you read this book, reflect on its words, and pray.

God's word, written or spoken, is like a mirror.[2] In a figurative sense, reason is the eye of your soul, and your conscience is your face. In the same way that you can't see an ugly pimple on your literal face without a mirror or someone else telling you about it, you can't find spiritual blemishes without using this mirror or hearing another's wise counsel. Unless you read or listen to God's word, it is impossible for the eyes of your understanding, blinded by the habit of sin, to see the grimy imperfection of your conscience.

And you react the same way in both instances. When you spot dirt on your face, whether you looked in a mirror or someone else told you about it—and I mean spiritually *or* literally—you run to any source of water and wash your face immediately. If this blemish is some particular sin already done, the fountain is the Holy Church and the water is a full confession. If it's only a secret root, an impulse to sin, then the wellspring is our merciful God and the water is profound prayer.

Let's review the three steps of preparation required of all beginners and intermediates who want to advance in contemplative prayer. First, read or listen to God's word. Next, reflect on it. Then, with this groundwork in place, real prayer can start.

36

Meditations of diligent contemplatives

Those diligent in their pursuit of contemplation have a different experience. Their meditations are sudden intuitions and an effortless consciousness. They don't have to read or hear Scripture first or meditate on anything special to trigger a sudden, secret awareness of their own sinfulness or of God's goodness. Such flashes of insight and simple awareness are better learned from God. No person can teach them.

At this point, as long as you feel moved by grace and have the approval of your spiritual director, I don't care if your meditations on your own sinfulness or on God's goodness are reduced to one simple word like _sin_ or _God,_ or any other you choose. But don't analyze these words or look up their etymologies. That clever display of wit won't increase your devotion. Your ability to reason is never helpful in contemplation.

Instead, embrace the word whole. If your word is

sin, focus on sin as a lump, impenetrable to your mind, but none other than yourself. I believe when you're engaged in this dark, simple awareness of sin as a hard lump (synonymous with you), there could be no more insane creature than you are then—you'll doubt your ability to live outside a strait jacket. But you won't look insane. No one will even guess you feel this way because your exterior will remain calm, and anyone looking at you will think all is well, since none of this inner turmoil is reflected in your face or body language. Sitting, walking, lying down, leaning, standing, or kneeling, you'll appear fully at ease, unruffled and restful.[1]

37

Personal prayers of diligent contemplatives

Just as the meditations of those skilled in contemplation come suddenly and directly, so do their prayers. I mean their personal prayers, not the liturgical prayers used in worship at church. True contemplatives value these community prayers above all others and participate in them as ordained by the Church and its earliest holy fathers. A contemplative's personal prayers, however, rise unrehearsed to God, with no go-betweens or specific ways of preparing.

Contemplatives seldom use words when they pray, but if they do, they choose only a few, and the fewer the better. They prefer a short one-syllable word over two syllables, because the spirit can best assimilate it. This one word keeps the person engaging in this spiritual exercise fit and at the top of their form, so to speak. Let me prove my point by telling a story from real life. When a person is terrified by a fiery catastrophe, someone's death, or something similar, they cry out for help. That's obvious. But what do they say? I can promise you a person in danger won't pray a long string of words or even a word of two syllables. Why not? When desperate, you've got no time to waste. At your wits' end and scared to death, there's no time for babbling or big words—you'll scream, "Fire!" or "Help!" and this one-word outburst works best.

Watch how this little word, "Fire!" penetrates a dangerous situation and gets the attention of those who can help you. The same is true spiritually. When a little word of one syllable is not just thought or spoken but is an expression of the deepest intentions of your spirit, it is the height of contemplation. (For the spirit, height and depth, length and breadth are all one place.) This simple prayer gets God's attention more quickly than any long Psalm mumbled mindlessly through closed teeth. That's why the Scriptures say, "A short prayer penetrates heaven."[1]

38

How and why a short prayer penetrates heaven

Why does this short little prayer of one small syllable penetrate heaven? Because you pray it with all that you are and all that you can be. This is the height and depth, length and breadth of your spirit, fully articulate. Through this one-word request, the spirit speaks its most powerful, highest prayer, because the deepest wisdom of your soul is contained in this single tiny word, which is also long in feeling, for if you could always experience that sense of urgency, you would sustain it and its genuine cry. Also, this one-word prayer expresses an inclusive, wide-reaching love, making you care for others and wish them everything you wish for yourself. As St. Paul says, this prayer will help you comprehend with all the saints the length, breadth, height, and depth of the everlasting, all-loving, all-powerful, and all-wise God, not fully but in part, in the dark way that is contemplative knowledge.[1]

The length of God is his everlasting nature, his

breadth is his love, his height is his power, and his depth is his wisdom. No surprise, then, that souls transformed by grace to the image and likeness of their Maker find God hears them immediately. God also hears sinful souls—technically his enemies—if, by grace, they can bring themselves to cry this one little syllable from the very height, depth, length, and breadth of their spirits. God always hears a shriek of pain and helps the soul in agony.

Let me give you an example. Imagine for a moment that you hear your worst enemy shouting, scared to death, "Fire!" or "Help!" You don't stop to ask, "Is that my enemy?" That one word stirs your compassion, and as the distressed cry rises, so do you. Even on a cold winter's night, you'll bolt from your chair, rushing to help put out a fire or to comfort your adversary. Dear Lord! If a mere person can be so utterly transformed by grace to show such mercy and sympathy for an enemy in need, overlooking dislike, what is God's mercy like when he hears our spirits crying out to him from the height and depth and length and breadth of our souls? Obviously there's no comparison, for God has more mercy than we can ever have. That's because God's mercy is who he is. It's his nature, and whatever mercy we possess we got by grace alone.

39

*Ways the experienced contemplative prays,
what prayer is, and which words most
contribute to the essence of prayer*

We are called to pray with an intensity reaching the height, depth, length, and breadth of our whole being. Also, when we pray, we shouldn't use many words but a little word of one syllable.

What word should you choose? Pick one best suited to the nature of prayer. Which word would that be? Before we discuss this, we should look at prayer. What is prayer? If we can answer that question, we can more clearly see which word best cultivates an attitude of prayer.

When understood properly, prayer is nothing but an intense longing for God, nurturing everything good and removing anything evil.

Since every evil is found in sin, either as a consequence or as the sin itself, when we want to pray wholeheartedly to get rid of evil, we should say, think, or mean this little word—*sin,* nothing else. No other words are needed. On the other hand, if we pray intently to get anything good, we should cry out in word, thought, or longing nothing but this word—*God,* nothing else. No other words are needed; for God's very nature is goodness, and he's the source of everything good.

Don't spend time wondering why I chose these two words over all of the others. I looked into it and found none better. If I had, or if God had taught me different ones, I would have chosen them over these, but I can think of no shorter words that so well represent everything good or everything evil. Follow my example. Don't analyze words at length because studying them isn't the same as doing the work of contemplative prayer. Only grace gives this gift.

So, even though I have recommended these two words, by all means select only the words God nudges you toward. However, if God moves you to take my two, stick with them and make them your own. That's my advice. I mean use them *if* you're praying with words, because their utter brevity is powerful. If you're not praying with words, that's fine, too.

Although I highly recommend short prayers, I'm not saying their frequency should be reduced. Pray simply and often. I've pointed out before that you're praying in the length of your spirit; therefore, don't stop your prayers until the thing you long for is achieved. We see an example of this in the frightened man or woman mentioned earlier. They won't stop shouting the little word, "Help!" or "Fire!" until someone comes to rescue them from trouble.

40

*That during contemplation a person does not
meditate on the nature of vice or virtue*

Do the same thing with the word *sin*. Saturate your soul
with its spiritual meaning without focusing on specifics
like the type of sin—venial or mortal—or what cate-
gory it belongs to—pride, anger, envy, greed, laziness,
gluttony, and lust.[1] What does it matter to a contemplative what kind of sin it is and how weighty? It's all
relative. This exercise teaches the contemplative how
large every sin is because even the smallest sin separates
us from God and prevents us from knowing true peace
of soul.

So feel sin as a lump, inscrutable to reason, but none
other than who you are. Then cry out in your spirit,
"Sin, sin, sin; help, help, help!" It's better for you to
learn this spiritual cry from God, by experience, than
from my all-too-human words. It's also best if you can
"shout" this word silently, without an actual thought or

sound. On rare occasions, however, your body and soul will fill to overflowing with the sorrow and burden of sin, and words may burst from you then.

Do the same with the little word *God*. Saturate your soul with its spiritual meaning without focusing on specifics like which of God's creations are good, better, or best, physical or spiritual, or on the virtues created by grace: humility, love, patience, abstinence, hope, faith, moderation, chastity, or voluntary poverty. What does any of that matter to contemplatives? They find and experience all virtues in God, in whom everything exists, for he creates all and is in all. Contemplatives understand that if they have God, they have everything good and need nothing else, so they desire nothing particularly, only the good God. Do this yourself, by grace. Be wholly intent on God, and only God, so nothing ever goes through your mind and heart but God alone.

That's why as long as you're living this mortal life, you'll always feel, one way or the other, this dirty, stinking lump of sin as an intrinsic part of your being, and that's why you must alternate your focus between these two words, *sin* and *God,* with this general understanding: if you possessed God, you would be sinless, and if you were sinless, you would have God.

41

That in everything except contemplation,
moderation is required

If you ask me what sort of self-control you need to do the work of contemplation, my answer is, "None at all!" In everything else you do, you should practice moderation. Avoid extremes when eating, drinking, or sleeping. Also, protect your body from severe cold or heat, don't pray or read too long, and don't spend too much time conversing with your friends. In all of these things, it's important that you do neither too much nor too little. But in contemplation you may throw caution to the wind. Indulge. I hope you'll never stop doing this loving work as long as you live.

I'm not saying that it's possible to keep the same high intensity all the time. You can't always keep your zest for contemplation. Sometimes you'll be sick or worn out mentally or physically, and sometimes life just intervenes, pulling you down and preventing you from scaling spiritual heights. That said, I advise you to stay at it. Stick to it, in all circumstances. I mean that when something intrudes and you can't practice contemplation, prepare for it still. Remain spiritually alert. So, for the love of God, try not to get sick. Discipline yourself as much as possible, so you won't be the cause of your own weakness. This work requires complete tranquillity and a healthy, pure disposition of body and soul. You must learn what rest is.

So, because you love God, take care of yourself. Stay as healthy as you can. But if illness comes your way in spite of your best efforts, be patient. Bear it with humility and wait on God's mercy. It will be enough; all will be well. Your patience in sickness and in dealing with different kinds of problems pleases God even more than the keenest devotion in times of good health.

42

*How an excess of contemplation helps a
person achieve balance in everything else*

You may want to know next how you can achieve a
balance in eating, drinking, sleeping, and in everything
else. In short, do the best you can. Work at contemplation, and you'll find your answer in it. Do it without
ceasing and without moderation. Indulge and never
stop, and it will teach you how to begin and when to
stop everything else you do. An "excess" of contemplation teaches self-control in every other activity. Abandon your soul to this work, persist in it night and day
without stopping, and you can't go wrong. But if you
don't devote yourself to it, you'll find yourself making
mistake after mistake in everyday matters.

If only my soul could wake up and always be attentive to this holy work, then I could experience a healthy
disregard for eating, drinking, sleeping, speaking, and
every other outward task. I really believe true moderation is possible if I can cultivate a beneficial indiffer-

ence toward these activities. Obsessively setting limits for these or analyzing each move I make won't help me become a balanced person. No matter how hard I might try, I don't think I can have success this way. Let other people say what they will, but their opinions fade in the light of experience.

So lift up your heart with a blind stirring of love. Focus on *sin* and then on *God*. You want to have God and lack sin, but you lack God and have sin. Now may our good God help you because you need him here.

43

*How you must absolutely lose all self-centered
knowledge and awareness before experiencing
the heights of contemplation*

Make sure you let nothing but God enter your mind or
work in your will. Try to reject any understanding or
feeling that is not God. Trample it down under the
cloud of forgetting. Then you'll see that in this work
you must not only forget all other creatures and their
actions, but also your own self and what you've done
for God. Watch how a true lover acts. When you are
perfect in love, you always love your beloved more
than yourself. In fact, in many ways you'll neglect yourself to serve the one you love.

That's how you should handle yourself. Loathe everything not God that crosses your mind or influences
your will. Grow weary of it, because—whatever it
is—it stands between you and God. Little wonder that
you hate thinking about yourself, because you have a

constant sense of your own sinfulness—that revolting, stinking, incomprehensible lump between you and God. And you know that lump is none other than you, inseparable from who you are, glued to your very essence.

So crush every thought of and feeling for every creature, especially thoughts and feelings for yourself. That's the linchpin. Your awareness of everything else is contingent on your awareness of yourself. Your reward for forgetting yourself is that you can then forget all other creatures easily. So try losing your self-consciousness. Test my advice, and you'll discover something remarkable. When you succeed in forgetting all creatures and their works and even your own life and all you've done, you will be left alone with God to experience a stark awareness of your own existence. But even this must go. Yes, you must lose the naked feeling of who you are. It must be destroyed, if you wish to experience the perfection of contemplation, or love.

44

How the soul can help destroy
its own self-centeredness

Next you'll ask me how you can destroy this basic
awareness of your self, perhaps because you're realizing
that if you can rid yourself of self-centeredness, all
other obstacles vanish, and you're right. My answer to
your question is twofold. Nothing happens without
God's generous gift of special grace, but the part you
play is equally important because you must be open to
receive his grace. Without both, your naked awareness
and experience of your being cannot be wiped out.

Your receptivity to God's grace is nothing but a
deep, powerful godly sorrow.[1] Be moderate. Don't be
harsh with yourself. Don't strain your body or soul. Sit
very still, as if asleep, exhausted and immersed in sorrow.[2] It's the best and truest grief on earth, and if you
do experience it, be grateful.

Everyone has reasons to be sad, but if you are someone who feels your existence deeply, you'll experience

sorrow in an especially profound way. Compared to this, every other sadness seems a charade. To be aware you're alive is genuinely painful, but if you're fortunate enough to feel not merely *who you are* but *that you are,* you understand more than others do why sorrow is universal and inescapable. Without experiencing godly sorrow, a person can never know real grief. If you lack that, weep to get it.

Godly sorrow cleanses the soul. It purifies the spirit, both of sin and of sin's shadow, which is suffering, and it readies the soul to receive the joy that snatches away your self-awareness. When your sorrow is genuine, it's a deep holy longing, full of sacred desires, or you would not be able to bear its intensity. And if you didn't have the joy of these desires feeding your soul during contemplation, you couldn't bear the pain of knowing and feeling *that you are.* Every time you long for a pure knowing and feeling of God (as far as is possible here) and find these blocked immediately because they are occupied and filled up by that repulsive, rancid lump of yourself, which must always be hated, despised, and forsaken if you want to be God's perfect disciple, as he taught on the mount of perfection,[3] this frustration can nearly drive you out of your mind with sorrow, weeping, lamenting, struggling, cursing, and self-accusation. To sum up, this burden of self can become so great that you no longer care what happens to it, as long as God is pleased.

But nowhere in this sorrow should you ever wish to not-be.[4] Thoughts of suicide are the devil's madness. They're a slap in God's face. We're meant to be grateful for the gift of life. God gave us this precious present. But it's also OK to wish with every moment that you could lose your awareness and feeling of your own being.

Godly sorrow and the deep longing it stirs in your soul are requirements for spiritual growth. If you'll open yourself up to God, he'll teach you these, in ways tailor-made for you. God's pedagogy is always personal. He wants only the best for you. If you are his student and he is your teacher, then you're also his friend. He knows the contour of your abilities and can teach you about love. Pay attention, and his grace will bind your soul to him in the joyful union of loving on earth as best as you can.

---

45

*A good explanation of certain hidden dangers
you may meet*

But I do want to warn you about one thing. A young disciple in contemplative prayer, inexperienced and unproven in this spiritual discipline, is easily deceived. So be careful. Stop, humble yourself, and seek good advice from a spiritual mentor, or you may be destroyed physically or spiritually. Don't practice prayer in such a way that you injure your body, and also don't let yourself be deluded. These problems come from pride, sensual cravings, and arrogant sophistry.

Here's how such mistakes can happen. Take a young man or woman who is new to this sort of thing. When beginners in the school of devotion hear lectures on godly sorrow and God-longing and are told to lift up their hearts to God with an unceasing desire to feel his love, sometimes their too-clever minds misinterpret this spiritual instruction superficially to mean that they should strain themselves physically and emotionally.

So they push their bodies to do the work that only grace can do. They're conceited and too inexperienced to know that intellectual vanity robs a person of grace and only leads to mental, physical, or emotional injury. But they think they can accomplish the work of contemplative prayer themselves, without grace, so they try and in a very short time, they exhaust themselves.

Their nervous systems strained and their bodies weakened, they cast about blindly for relief, turning to empty pleasures of the flesh and other material comforts. Their road from contemplation to recreation is short. If this doesn't happen, sometimes their spiritual obtuseness and physical self-abuse overstimulate them to the point of whipping their souls into a frenzy instead. This is not true contemplative prayer. It's something bogus, the work of our spiritual enemy, the devil, and it is caused by feelings of self-importance, a love of being praised, undisciplined passions, and smug minds.

The problem is that these beginners believe that their experience is the real deal. They mistake a high-strung excitement and warmth in their cheeks for the genuine fire of love kindled by the grace and goodness of the Holy Spirit deep within our hearts. This counterfeit experience causes many problems and much suffering. It has terrible consequences because it stirs up much hypocrisy, heresy, and error. For those being educated by the devil, each phony experience leads to false knowledge, just as each genuine experience of God's teaching leads to true knowledge. I'm telling you straight—the devil has his own contemplatives, just as God does. Also, pseudo-contemplative experiences and their unbelievable, wrong knowledge are as varied as each human is uniquely surprising in temperament and lifestyle. That's equally true for those who practice real contemplative prayer. It's different for each individual.

But I think I've told you enough, so I won't describe more potential problems of this sort. I've covered those that I believe you'll encounter in this work, if you decide to pursue it. You'll be attacked in these ways and must be ready to meet them. I don't think, however, that you need to read about all of the other temptations and mistakes made by the most learned theologians and by others from backgrounds unlike yours. What good would that do? Trust me, none. So I stop here.

46

---

*How to escape these hidden dangers and
practice contemplation with a joyful spirit,
rather than brute force*

So, for the love of God, guard against these dangers.
And don't be hard on yourself. By that, I mean don't
overtax yourself emotionally or physically. Choose to
be enthusiastic instead. This discipline doesn't require
brute strength, but joy. As you increase the joy in your
contemplative work, you also increase its humility and
genuine spirituality, but if you force it, your efforts sink
into a crude physicality. So beware. Remember that
anyone approaching the high mountain of contemplation with a beastly heart will be driven away with
stones.[1]

You know that stones are hard, dry things and that
they hurt when they strike you. In the same way, harsh
straining in contemplative work is hard on our bodies
and emotions, and it also has the sheer dryness that
results when the dew of grace is absent. So when these

"stones" of inflexibility and overexertion strike the fool-ish[2] soul, they hurt it through and through, leaving spiritual sores, where hellish delusions fester. That's why you should be careful. Instead of being stubborn as a mule, learn to love with gentleness and joy, kind-ness and good manners.

Cultivate self-control of body and soul. Accept the will of our Lord gracefully. Never lunge for it like a hungry dog. Even if you're starving, don't be a greedy greyhound. Don't grab. Let me suggest how you can do this. I'm going to advise you to play a sort of game with God, seriously. Pretend you don't want what you want as much as you want it. When you feel that beast, desire, stirring inside you with tremendous power, restrain it. Act as if you don't want God to find out how much you long to see him, know him, and feel him. Hide all that.

Perhaps I sound like a child making up a game, but I mean it. I'm confident that anyone with the grace to put my advice into practice will eventually experience the joy of God's playfulness. God will come to you, the way an earthly father plays with his child, kissing and hugging, making everything alright.[3]

47

Wise words teaching purity of spirit in contemplative prayer and the difference between showing our desire to God and to others

---

Don't be surprised that I speak in what seems like a "childish" and foolish way, as if I'm lacking in sense, for I have my reasons. For some time now, I've been led[1] to feel, think, and speak in this way to some other special friends in God, and now to you.

Here's one reason you should hide the longing of your heart from God. He sees the yearning you hide more clearly than what you bare, and your desire is fulfilled more quickly. There's no better way of "showing" him what you want. Here's another reason I believe this approach works. Learning to conceal what you wish revealed will wean you from a dependence on your fragile, fickle human emotions and deepen the purity of your spiritual awareness. Finally, this way helps you tie the spiritual knot of burning love between you and God in a mystical oneness of wills.

You're well aware that God is spirit, so the person who wants to be united with him must have a profound sincerity of spirit, without pretense. It's true that God is omniscient, and nothing physical or spiritual can be hidden from his mind, but, because God is spirit, the most obvious, open petition is whatever lies hidden in the depths of your spirit, rather than anything emotional or otherwise tainted by the senses. He has an affinity with our souls, so when we panic and get stressed, straining our emotions and our bodies, we are not close to God. We're much better off when we devote ourselves to finding joy in the work of contemplative prayer and practicing it serenely, with purity and deep wisdom.

I hope my explanation helps you understand why I'm asking you to cover and hide the longing of your heart from God, like a child playing a game. I'm not, however, asking you to hide it completely. Only an idiot would ask you to do that, because it's impossible. But I'm still saying try your best—do all you can to hide it from God. Why do I ask you this? I want you to cast[2] your longing deep in your spirit, far from anything corrupt, which would make it less spiritual and further from God. I know that as your soul grows in purity of spirit, your desires become less emotional and your soul draws nearer to God. And as your soul pleases him more, he can see it more clearly. I'm not saying that God sees better sometimes than others, for his vision is the same yesterday, today, and forever; but your soul resembles God more when it is pure in spirit because God is spirit.

I have one more reason for asking you to do all that you can to conceal your desire from God. You and I, plus many others like us, are prone to literal interpretations of spiritual realities. I was afraid that if I asked you to show your heart's desire to God, you might understand this physically and try articulating it with a look, an intonation, a word, a gesture, or some other human way, as you do when sharing your most intimate thoughts with a friend here on earth. But that approach would only make your contemplative work worldly. For we reveal confidences to our human friends one way, but when we show them to God, we must take a totally different approach.

---

48

*How God wants you to serve him physically and
spiritually, how he rewards both, and how he
helps you discern between good and evil spiritual
delights during contemplation*

I'm not trying to discourage you from praying aloud.
And I don't want you to feel that you can't burst into
words when your spirit fills to overflowing and you're
moved to talk to God as you would to a friend, saying
things like, "Good Jesus! Lovely Jesus! Sweet Jesus!"
and others. No, God forbid you understand me to mean
that. That's not at all what I intend. And God forbid
that I'd ever attempt to separate body and spirit, which
God has joined together. Both serve him, as is right,
and both are rewarded, too.

Sometimes he gives his friends a foretaste of that
eternal reward. He may set their senses on fire, not just
once or twice in this life, but sometimes quite often,
whenever he wishes. When this happens, they feel an
ineffable sweetness and an intense delight. Their plea-

sure doesn't come from outside the body, entering through the windows of our intellect; it comes from within, waking in our souls and bubbling up from an abundance of joy and true devotion of spirit. There's no need to be suspicious of this comfort and this delight. Once you've experienced it, I think you'll understand why I say that.

But mistrust all other consolations, sounds, gladness, and sweet ecstasies that come suddenly and externally, from sources you can't identify. They can be good or evil. If they're good, they are the work of a good angel, and if they're evil, they are the work of an evil angel. The spiritual delights that you experience will never be evil as long as you remember what I've taught you and follow my teaching (or if you can find better instruction on this point, follow it). Avoid the devil's deceptive, false way of thinking and undisciplined, excessive straining of body and soul. Why? Because then the source of your comfort is certain—it will be that devout stirring of love making its home in the pure heart, created by the hand of almighty God, without any intermediary. So it exists far from every illusion and untrustworthy opinion humans can hold.

Right now I won't cover how you can distinguish whether the other consolations, sounds, and delights are good or evil. I don't think it's necessary, since you can find that outlined for you in another man's book, where it's described a thousand times better than I ever could.[1] His work is much better than anything I've written. But what does that matter? I write what I write anyway, for I want to discuss the discipline of contemplation with you. It's no trouble for me to answer the longings and questions of your heart, which you first made clear in your words and now make evident in your actions.

But I will say this to you about the harmonies and pleasures that come in by the windows of your intellect and may be good or may be evil. Always exercise yourself in this blind, heartfelt, joyful longing of love that is contemplation, and I have no doubt that it will tell you all about them and teach you to distinguish which is which. If you're somewhat astonished at first by these strange and unfamiliar spiritual delights, contemplative prayer will help you with them because it binds your heart and keeps you calm, giving you the presence of mind to wait. You won't endorse these until they've been fully approved, either from within by God's wonderful Spirit, or from without, on the advice of some discerning spiritual mentor.

49

That the essence of all perfection is nothing but a good will, and how every possible comfort in this life is nonessential

So I encourage you—bow eagerly to love. Follow its humble stirrings in your heart. Let it guide you in this life, and it will bring you safely to eternal bliss in the next. Love is the essence of all goodness. Without it, no kind work is ever begun or finished. Simply put, love is a good will in harmony with God. When you have it, you get supreme satisfaction and joy from everything he does.

This good will is the essence of every perfection. The delights and consolations of body and soul, no matter how holy, are incidental to this good will and dependent on it. I call them "incidental" because they're nonessential; their absence or presence doesn't affect love. In this life, we can live without them, but in eternity, they are indivisible from our joy, just as the body will be totally united with the soul then. Here on earth, we know these consolations spiritually, in the goodness of our will and in the joy that it brings us. I'm equally certain that the mature contemplative who has perfected his or her will (as far as is possible here on earth) is just as happy to do without worldly delights and consolations as to have them, if that's what God wants.

50

What pure love is, and how some contemplatives rarely experience tangible consolations, while others feel them often

Now I'm sure you see why it's important that we focus our attention wholly on this humble stirring of love in the will. As for every other physical delight or spiritual gift, no matter how wonderful or how holy, I say with all due respect that we should take no notice of them. If they come, welcome them, but don't lean on them much, for fear of becoming weak. It takes too much of your energy to linger any length of time in such sweet feelings and tears. And you might begin to love God— not for himself alone, as you should—but for these. You'll know that's the case if their absence makes you irritable and grouchy. If this is your experience, then you'll know that your love is not pure or perfect. A mature love has already had its dependency on such delights purified. When gentle emotions and tears come, an experienced love accepts them for the nourishment and comfort they provide the body's senses, but it doesn't grumble when they're missing because it's genuinely happy not to have them, if that's God's will.

Some contemplatives experience these consolations as a matter of course, others rarely. That's entirely up to God. He knows our diverse needs and decides what best benefits each of us. Some people are so spiritually fragile and tenderhearted that they must be reassured by pleasant feelings or they could never endure the many temptations and problems that burden them in this life. Without these comforts, they simply would not have the strength to deal with their physical and spiritual adversaries. And some people have such frail bodies that they can't endure rigorous physical acts of penance for cleansing, but our Lord is gracious and purifies them through feelings of sweet consolation and tears. On the other hand, some people are so strong in spirit that they gather all the comfort they need inside their souls as they offer up this heartfelt, humble stirring of love with an obedient will. This alone is their comfort, and they don't much need any other. Which of these ways is holier or dearer to God? Only God knows. I don't.

51

---

*That we must be careful not to interpret
literally something meant spiritually,
especially the words* in *and* up

So bow to love, humbly. Follow its blind stirrings in
your heart. I don't mean your physical heart but your
spiritual heart, which is your will. Be careful not to
interpret literally what I mean spiritually. Believe me
when I tell you that people with overly sophisticated,
overly imaginative minds can have ideas that cause
much error.

Think for a minute about my asking you to conceal
your desire from God as much as possible. Perhaps if I
had said, "Show your desire to God," you would have
understood this advice far more literally than when I
say, "Hide it," because you know that deliberately hid-
ing anything means that you have to fling it deep into
your spirit.

This warning is so important that I feel I must reiter-
ate it. When we hear words spoken in a spiritual sense,

we must be careful how we interpret them. When something is meant to be understood figuratively, we shouldn't take it literally. For example, look at the words *in* and *up*. These two words are often misunderstood by those setting out to be spiritually active as contemplatives, and their distorted meanings create much error and illusion. I know this partly from experience and partly from what others have told me. I'll tell you a little about these fallacies.

Young disciples in God's school, having only recently rejected the world and having only spent a short time in penance and prayer under the guidance of a spiritual advisor, feel totally prepared for contemplation. These beginners have certainly heard others speak or read aloud on this topic, or they may have read about contemplation privately. But what do novices really know of contemplative prayer? Immediately, our undiscerning beginners misunderstand what they hear or read about this discipline such as, "the contemplative must concentrate inwardly, drawing together every mental resource within" and "must climb up, rising above self." Hearing this, those ignorant of the interior life find their sensuality and natural curiosity take over, and they feel a lust to uncover secrets and so believe that they are "called" to do the work of contemplation. If a spiritual director disagrees, saying, "No, you're not called to this work," the disgruntled student will often seek out others with the same point of view, complaining to them, "Nobody understands me."

Arrogance and overconfidence overwhelm the good judgment of these contemplative novices. They stop the humble work of prayer and penance too soon, to charge off in the direction of what they think is contemplation, but their spiritual exercises are not genuine. Instead, their "contemplation" is something freakish. It goes against nature, with the devil in charge, and it's the quickest way to death of body and soul. This is insanity, not wisdom, and can drive a person crazy. Worst of all, its practitioners don't know that. They believe their contemplative mission is clear and are resolved to think on nothing but God.

_____

How arrogant young disciples misunderstand
in and are then tricked

_____

Here's how the disciples' insanity happens. Beginners read and hear that they should give up use of their external senses and only work interiorly, but they don't know what "work interiorly" means, so they get it all wrong. What they do next is unnatural. They strain at introspection. They try to make their physical eyes see spiritually, their physical ears hear interiorly, and so on with all of their senses. They try to smell, taste, and feel their souls. This reversal of nature has violent repercussions, and when it's combined with a curiosity that overexerts the imagination, they "flip out."[1]

This mistake opens the door to the devil, who invents illusions of light and sound; sweet fragrances in their noses; delicious tastes in their mouths; bizarre, intense emotions; and strange burning sensations and passions in their bodies, spreading through their breasts, bowels, backs, groins, and private parts. But they are deluded, believing they've achieved a peaceful mind, totally focused on God, with no distracting thoughts. I suppose they have, in a way, because they're so full of falseness that pride can't harm them. Why is that? The perpetrator of this work is the same devil who'd be sending them distracting thoughts if their prayers were genuine, and you know perfectly well that the devil is not going to get in the way of his own crime. So he leaves them their awareness of God, because if he took that away from them, he fears they might get suspicious.

---

*The various offensive mannerisms of those
who call themselves contemplatives but
aren't really doing the work of this book*

Pseudo-contemplatives are prone to the oddest behavior, because they've deceived themselves. On the other hand, God's genuine disciples have good manners and are modest, too. That's not true of counterfeit contemplatives. If you could watch them sitting in contemplation, eyes open, you'd see how they stare straight ahead, as if crazy, and they grin as though they see the devil. And it's good that they're on the lookout, for he's not far away. Some have eyes frozen in place, like the eyes of sheep that suffer from sturdy[1] and have been knocked in the head and will soon die. Some let their heads hang to one side, as if a worm were in their ears. Some squeak when they speak, as if they had no breath; they sound like hypocrites. Some always shout and clear their throats, greedy to speak, in a hurry to get their points across. Heretics act like this, and so do clever, arrogant people stubbornly holding to wrong ways of thinking.

If you could see everything these fake contemplatives do, you'd witness lots more of this grotesque, indecent behavior. Believe it or not, some are smart enough to control themselves in public, but if you could be with them at home, with their guard down, you'd see their true colors. I also believe that if you were ever bold enough to contradict them on anything, you'd see their bubble of control burst as they lash out at you in anger. Yet, they think that everything they do is for the love of God and supports his truth. If God does not intervene in their lives with a miracle of mercy, I think they will continue "loving God" in this fashion until they go straight to the devil, stark mad. I'm not saying that the devil has a perfect slave who is deceived and infected by every fantasy I've described here, though that wouldn't be entirely impossible, either, for maybe even more than one person. What I am saying is that no hypocrite or heretic is complete without some of the pretenses I've described or will now describe to you, God willing.

These strange, unhealthy mannerisms handicap some people so much that they listen in a superficial way, twisting their heads to one side and pointing their chins up at you, mouths wide open, as if they could hear you with that hole, instead of with their ears. Some can't speak without pointing their fingers for emphasis, rapping their palms, tapping their own chests for emphasis, or even poking the chests of those they're lecturing. Some can't be still. They fidget. They're restless sitting, standing, and lying down. Their feet don't ever stop moving, and their hands must always be doing something. When some talk, they make rowing motions with their arms, as if they're trying to swim across an ocean. Some smile and laugh constantly, at every other word, hungry for attention. They prostitute themselves in any way they can, clowning, always cracking rude jokes and stirring up trouble wherever they go.[2] It's much better to choose a modest face, humble behavior, and a gracious joy.

I'm not saying that these outrageous mannerisms are themselves terrible sins or that those who act this way are great sinners. But if these indecorous, disorderly behaviors gain the upper hand and a person becomes addicted to them, then I do believe they are an indication of arrogance, intellectual dishonesty, exhibitionism, and a greedy mind. Worst of all, they are signs of emotional instability and an anxious soul, which develop in the absence of true contemplative work. The only reason I have described these problems here is so that contemplatives can test the genuine nature of their work against them.

54

*How contemplation makes a person wise
and attractive, physically and spiritually*

Everyone who practices contemplation finds that this
loving work has a good influence on both body and soul.
It helps them get themselves in hand, and this, in turn,
makes them attractive to others they meet. Even the
ugliest man or woman engaged in this spiritual discipline discovers its grace completely transforms them.
Outer appearances are altered. Good people are drawn
to experienced contemplatives and enjoy their company. In the presence of those who have steeped their
lives in the discipline of contemplation, others feel
peace and through grace are brought closer to God.

So seek this gift, and let grace help you. Those who
have it learn to control themselves and their lives
through it. When necessary, you'll have the discernment to read the temperaments and needs of everyone
you meet. You'll also develop a knack for identifying
with and making yourself at home with anyone, even

stubborn sinners, without losing your essential person-hood or falling into sin yourself—to the amazement of all. And through God's grace, your gentle spirit will draw others to the work of contemplation.

Too, if you're a true contemplative, your life and words will overflow with spiritual wisdom, compassion, and fruitful insight, because you're sure to measure out what you say carefully and calmly, eschewing lies and speaking without the shrill pretense of hypocrites. However, some people are so insecure that they focus all of their energy on their reputations, so they deliberately inject their conversations with humble-sounding words and fake loving gestures. You know them, and you know they only want to look holy in the sight of others. They could care less how God and his angels view them. When these people make a single social blunder in public, they get more upset and embarrassed by this insignificant mistake than they do for deliberately thinking a thousand arrogant thoughts or indulging in countless impure impulses in full view of God and every saint and angel in heaven. Ah, Lord God! People churning out copious words of false humility give much away, for these are really the spoors of hidden pride. Yes, of course, the truly humble should speak and act modestly, always, but that's totally different from the fake emotion and broken voice and feeble, trembling tones of hypocrites, who sound so totally unlike themselves. Sincere words are spoken simply. Words, voice, and spirit are one. But here's what hypocrisy looks like. When a person with a steady, booming voice affects humility by stammering in a harsh, forced whisper—unless that person is sick or talking alone with God or to a confessor—it's an obvious sign of duplicity. And don't let age fool you. Hypocrites may be old as well as young.

What else should I say of this toxic phoniness? I truly believe that unless grace helps these miserable souls stop their shrill hypocrisy, they'll soon drown in the despair created by the inner pride of their hearts and the outer modesty of their words.

---

*That people are mistaken when they
indiscreetly and zealously rebuke sin*

Our adversary also deceives some in another way. He
sets their brains on fire for God, so to speak, giving
them an unbounded passion for protecting divine law
by destroying sin in others. The devil won't tempt them
with anything obviously evil; instead, he makes them
act like zealous church leaders[1] keeping watch over
every aspect of our Christian life or like an abbot over-
seeing his monks. These people criticize all people for
their faults, as if they were really pastors, legally responsible for the care of others' souls.[2] They believe
God requires this from them and that they dare not
stop. Then they say that God's love and a desire to help
others moves them to point out others' imperfections,
but they lie. The fire of hell has ignited their brains and
their imaginations.

What follows confirms this. The devil is a spirit. He
does not have a body, and the same is true of angels.

That said, whenever God allows him or an angel to assume a body to interact with someone on earth, that form takes the shape of the spirit's mission. We find examples of this truth in sacred Scripture. We read in the Old and New Testaments that when an angel was sent out to do God's work, its name, abilities, or something about its body revealed the angel's spiritual message. It's also true with the devil. When he takes on human form, some quality of that body betrays his demonic intentions.

One example suffices. I've learned from students of necromancy, who conjure evil spirits, and from those to whom the devil has appeared in physical form, that when he assumes any human shape, he only has one nostril, and it's fat and wide.[3] And he's always willing to flare it up at people so they can get a good look at his brain, which is nothing but the fire of hell, and he likes nothing better than convincing people to look up there, because when they see it, they lose their minds forever. Of course, the highly skilled student of necromancy knows this already and takes the necessary steps to prevent such danger.

That's why I say, as I've said before, that when the devil takes a human shape, some quality of that body betrays his demonic intentions. He inflames the imagination of his contemplatives with hellfire, until suddenly, with no forethought and without any tact, they launch attacks on others. They never lack presumption, but criticize people in the most arbitrary fashion. That's because, spiritually speaking, they only have one nostril. Consider the septum inside a person's nose. This membrane separates one nostril from the other, symbolizing the discretion each person should develop spiritually. People with this strength learn to distinguish good from evil, bad from worse, and good from better, before passing judgment on anything they've heard or seen. (A person's imagination is naturally located and functions in the head, and that's what I mean, in a spiritual sense, when I refer to the "brain"—I mean that person's imagination.)

56

---

*How hypocrisy occurs when people rely more on
their own cleverness and education than on the
gospel teaching and counsel of the Holy Church*

Though some people never blunder into the delusions
I've just described, they still let their pride, intellectual
curiosity, and erudition lead them away from the gospel, its teaching, and the counsel of the holy Church.
They and their friends trust their own opinions too
much.[1] They have not grounded themselves in the
humble, blind experience of contemplative love, so
they don't know how good life can be. They deserve a
shallow, deluded existence, a superficial life filled with
the devil's tricks. Eventually, these people will ex-
plode. They'll blaspheme and disown the saints, sacra-
ments, commands, and ceremonies of the holy Church.
Worldly people, assuming that the divine teachings of
the church are too hard to follow for spiritual transformation, turn immediately (and without thinking) to
these heretics, giving them their full support, because

they think that these fanatics will take them down an easier path than the church will.

I truly believe that those who don't choose the arduous, disciplined way to heaven will lope downhill to hell.[2] Find this out for yourself. If we could see heretics and their followers as they'll appear on the Last Day, we would see how burdened they are by the world's most horrifying sins, by their own secretly indulged physical passions, and by their open presumption in following error. It's quite right that they're called the disciples of the Antichrist, because, as often noted, though they have the appearance of public virtue, their private lives are dedicated to the shameful pleasures of lust.

How arrogant young disciples misunderstand
up *and are then tricked*

But enough of this for now, let's go back to our discussion of the word *up*. I mentioned earlier that beginners often misunderstand its meaning. That's because they're rushed, and when they hear someone read or preach that we must "lift up our hearts to God," right away they look up at the stars as if they wish to travel beyond the moon and cock their ears in that direction, as if they could hear the angels singing in heaven. Sometimes they decide to use their clever imaginations to penetrate the mysteries of the planets and make a hole in the firmament to look through.[1] They make God in the shape of their desires, covering him in expensive clothes and placing him on a throne, creating a mental image far more fantastic than any painting done of him on earth. They also give angels human shapes and different kinds of musical instruments—most odd!

The devil deceives some of these people surprisingly well. He sends a sort of dew that they mistake for the food of angels. It seems to appear from nowhere, falling gently from the air and landing sweetly in their mouths. That's why they develop the habit of sitting with their mouths agape, as if waiting to catch flies. Obviously this is nothing but an illusion. Never mind that it looks holy. While all of this is going on, their souls are empty, lacking genuine devotion while their hearts are filled with the self-worship and dishonesty of their weird spiritual "exercises." In fact, sometimes the devil fakes odd sounds in their ears, strange lights shining in their eyes, and lovely smells in their noses. It's all a lie.

But they don't believe that. They think it's all genuine and are fully convinced that they're merely following the examples set by St. Martin, St. Stephen, and others, who were completely devoted to the "looking upward" of contemplative love. Once, when St. Martin was practicing contemplation, he looked up and had a revelation in which he saw God, surrounded by angels, and wearing his robe. St. Stephen saw our Lord standing up in heaven, and Christ ascended up to heaven in his human body, as his disciples watched. That's why they say we should turn our eyes upward. I completely agree that if we feel moved during worship, we should lift up our flesh-and-blood eyes and hands, but I believe just as strongly that when we do the work of the spirit, we don't actually move up or down or from side to side or forward or backward. Contemplative love has no up, down, left, right, front, or back. We experience it spiritually, unlimited by physical dimensions.

58

That we should not view the lives of St. Martin
and St. Stephen as literal examples of how to
strain our imaginations upward
during contemplation

Yes, it's true what they say about St. Martin and St. Stephen. They did see such things with their physical eyes, but these miracles were granted them for teaching spiritual truths. Obviously St. Martin's robe was never really worn by Christ because he had no need to be protected from cold weather, but St. Martin saw his robe on Christ so that this miraculous image could instruct us along the way of salvation and help us be united with the spiritual body of Christ. It was a symbol of Christ's teaching, for whoever clothes someone in need or does any other good deed for the love of God, certainly does it to Christ in spirit, and they will be rewarded as if they had done that kindness to Christ's own human body. He says that in the Gospel,[1] but he felt this was not enough and wanted to prove his teaching. So he gave St. Martin this miraculous vision.

Every earthly revelation has a spiritual significance. I believe that if we humans were more spiritual, we wouldn't need visions. These are given whenever someone hasn't quite grasped an invisible spiritual lesson and needs a visual to go with it. We must learn to pull off this rough husk and feed on its sweet kernel.

But how? Not like the heretics, that's for sure. They act like wild men who, after drinking from a splendid cup, have the custom of hurling it against a wall and smashing it. We won't imitate their crass behavior. Such excess gets us nowhere, and we want our souls to grow. We aim to do well spiritually. We won't cram our faces so full of fruit that we despise the tree, and we won't drink so much that we break the cup that held the drink.

Here's what I mean. The tree and the cup represent visible miracles and every helpful physical movement we make that advances the work of the spirit, such as lifting our eyes and our hands up to heaven. The fruit and the drink symbolize the underlying spiritual meaning of these visible miracles and devotional gestures. If our actions are animated by God's Spirit, they will always be authentic; but if they aren't, they will be fake and hypocritical. When genuine, they contain spiritual fruit, so why scorn them? Remember that people kiss the cup, grateful for the wine it holds.

What are we supposed to learn from our Lord's physical ascension into heaven? Much is made of his traveling up through the clouds as his mother and disciples watched with their earthly eyes. Does that give us the license in contemplative spiritual work to stare upward with our physical eyes, always looking to see if we can catch a glimpse of Jesus sitting or standing in heaven, as St. Stephen did? I don't think so. Clearly God did not show St. Stephen this vision in order to recommend that we scan heaven with our earthly eyes, hoping to see Jesus up there standing, sitting, or lying down. No one knows how his body looks in heaven. Plus, we don't need to know. We only need to know that his body is exalted and united there with his soul, forever. His body and his soul represent his humanity, and they are united there with his divinity, indivisibly. We really don't need to know if he sits or stands or reclines. Instead, rest in this knowledge—in heaven, Jesus does as he likes, and his body exists in whatever way is best for him. Whenever he shows himself to someone as reclining, standing, or sitting, this is only done to teach a spiritual truth, not to indicate how he really moves and acts in heaven.

Here's an example of what I mean. "Standing" represents a readiness to help. Friends say this to each other. We "stand" by each other. Before a battle, one friend says to another: "Have courage. Fight hard, and don't give in to fear. Don't quit, for I'll stand by you."

That faithful friend doesn't just mean a physical "standing," because the battle may be fought on horseback and not on foot. In fact, the "standing" by may happen in a moving cavalry charge. Whenever someone says "I'll stand by you," they mean, "I'm here and ready to help you."

That's why our heavenly Lord appeared "standing" in a vision to St. Stephen, to comfort him as he was being martyred, to show that he was spiritually "standing by" him. This vision is not a recommendation that we should always be raising our earthly heads and looking up to heaven when we pray. Instead, it's as if God were saying to St. Stephen and to all those like him who have suffered for loving: "Look, Stephen. Just as I can open the firmament of heaven and let you see me standing there in my body, trust that I'm standing by you spiritually, with the strength of my divinity. I'm ready to help you. So stand strong in the faith. Suffer boldly as the cruel stones strike you, for I'll crown you in eternal joy. You and everyone suffering for me and my love will be rewarded."

So you see these physical visions were given by grace to reveal spiritual truths.

————

59

*That we should also not view Christ's ascension
as a literal example of how our imaginations
should be strained upward during contemplation,
and that when we are engaged in contemplative
work, time, place, and the body must be forgotten*

————

If you argue that our Lord's ascension was actually meant to teach us both a spiritual *and* a physical lesson because he ascended to heaven in a physical body, genuinely both God and man, I would counter that he had been dead and was resurrected at the time, that his body was already transformed, clothed in immortality.[1] The same will happen to us on the Day of Judgment. We'll be so refined in body and soul then that together they'll create a mysterious, sublime new form, and in this imperishable "body" we will be able to travel as swiftly as thought. As quickly as you can think "up" or "down," this new "body" will move up or down, from one side to the other, and backward and forward. Everything will be equally easy, and all will be good, as the theologians say.[2] But right now you can't get to heaven physically, only spiritually, and your contemplative work will be so spiritual that it will resemble nothing physical. In contemplation, direction as we know it ceases to exist. *Up, down, to, from, behind,* and *before* vanish.

It's true, despite the fact that we use such words to describe the contemplative exercises outlined in this book. Those doing the spiritual work discussed here must remember that when they read phrases like, "lift *up*" and "go *in,*" these aren't meant physically, and when we call contemplation a "stirring," we don't mean this word literally. That said, we're required to be fully active in contemplative work, spiritually "stirring," but this stirring is not a physical reaching upward or inward or a motion from one place to another. Even when contemplation is sometimes called a "rest," that term doesn't mean "staying in one place and not moving away." When done maturely, this work is so pure and spiritual that, if you could see it for what it truly is, you'd know it's far removed from motion and location.

We'd be better off referring to contemplation as a sudden change rather than as anything to do with any geographical location because time, place, and body must be forgotten during this spiritual work. So beware of viewing Christ's ascension as a literal example of how our imaginations should strain upward during contemplation, as if you could climb over and beyond the moon. That's not spiritual. If you could ascend to heaven as Christ did, then, yes, you could use the ascension as an example, but you can't do that. Only God can. He himself confirmed this truth, saying, "No one has ascended into heaven except the one who descended from heaven, the Son of Man, who became human for the love of humanity."[3] Even if it were possible for us to ascend physically into heaven (and it isn't), this movement could only occur through an excess of spiritual work and its power and would have nothing whatsoever to do with any physical exertion or straining of our own imaginations in any direction, whether up or in or from side to side. So have nothing to do with this fallacy. It's irrelevant.

60

*That the quickest, best way to heaven
is measured by desires, not by feet*

And now perhaps you ask, "But how can that be?" You
think you have absolute proof that heaven is in the direction of *up,* since Christ, when he ascended into
heaven, went *up;* and later, as promised, he sent the
Holy Spirit down from *above,* as all of his disciples witnessed this gift.[1] Yes, we believe this. So you ask why,
on the strength of this evidence, shouldn't you direct
your mind literally upward during contemplative
prayer?

I'll answer you as well as my weakness permits.
Since Christ ascended in physical form and then after-
ward sent the Holy Spirit physically, it was more fitting
that his journey to heaven was described as "up" rather
than "down" and that the Holy Spirit's path to earth
was described as "from above" rather than "from below," "from behind," "in front of," or "on one side or

another." I say that it was "more fitting" because it makes more sense to us, but in reality, the direction—that he went up instead of down—didn't matter, since it's all the same distance. Spiritually speaking, heaven is as close down as up, as close behind as before, as quickly reached from one side as the other.

In fact, anyone who longs for heaven is already there in spirit. The highway to heaven is measured by desires, not by feet. Our longing is the most direct route. That's why St. Paul says this about himself and others: "Although our bodies are presently here on earth, our home is in heaven."[2] He's describing the world of the spirit and how on earth we must make our home in love and right desire. If you want to find your soul, look at what you love. That's where your soul lives, just as it lives in your body, giving it life.[3] And that's why if we want to go to heaven spiritually, we don't need to strain our spirits in any direction, up or down or from one side to another. Whenever we love, we're already there.

61

That when nature follows God's rules,
flesh is subject to spirit, and not the reverse

That said, it helps if we lift our physical eyes and hands up to the literal heavens, where God has fixed the stars and all of the planets. I mean that we should do this only if we're moved by the Spirit during contemplative work, because every physical thing is subject to and ruled by something spiritual, never the reverse.

We see an example of this truth in our Lord's ascension. When the ordained time came, and it pleased him to physically return to his Father in his humanity (which never was and never could be separated from his divinity), through the power of God's almighty Spirit, his humanity and body traveled physically as one person, and it was fitting that the mystery of his journey was made visible by an upward movement.

When we practice the spiritual exercises described in this book, we can learn more about the submission of body to spirit. When your soul conscientiously focuses on this loving work, immediately and often without knowing it, your body follows the lead of your interior activity. If at first your body was bent down or to one side so that you could be more comfortable, during contemplation God's Spirit gives your body the power to stand up straight, erect. Your body imitates your soul and makes the work of the Spirit evident. That's how it always is.

And that's why humans (the most beautiful creatures God made) weren't created facing the earth like the other beasts; instead, we were made upright, facing heaven. Our bodies physically reflect the spiritual work that our souls were made to do. Spiritually, God designed us for uprightness, not for crookedness. Notice that I mean *upright* in a spiritual sense, for how can the immateriality that is the soul ever strain itself to stand upright in a physical sense? No, that's not possible.

So be careful. Don't take spiritual truths literally, even though they're described with familiar words like *up* or *down, in* or *out, behind* or *ahead,* and *on one side* or *another*. We can't not use these physical metaphors. No matter how spiritual something is, if we want to discuss it—since speech is a physical act made by the tongue that is part of the body—obviously we must use physical words. But how do we understand these? Do we take them literally? No, we learn to understand them spiritually.

62

How to know when your spiritual work
concerns what is outside and beneath you,
when it is inside you and on your level,
and when it is above you but under God

It would help you, I think, if I explained the spiritual meanings of some of the ordinary terms used in contemplative work. Then you'll understand their figurative significance, and this knowledge will make it easier for you to avoid error and better grasp when your spiritual activity is outside and below you, when it is within you and on your level, and when it is above you but under God.

Everything material is naturally outside your soul and below you. Yes, this is even true of the sun, moon, and stars. Though they shine above your literal head, they're inferior to or "below" your soul. On the other hand, the angels and souls transformed and made beautiful by grace and virtues are "above" or superior to you in purity, but they're still equal with you in the natural order. Next, if you look within, you'll see that nature has gifted you with three principal powers of the soul: mind, reason, and will, and two secondary ones: imagination and sensuality. In nature's hierarchy, God alone comes above you.

From now on, whenever you come across the word *yourself* in spiritual books, remember that it refers to your soul, not to your body, and that your contemplative work is judged on the merit of your soul's focus in it. The contours and worth of your contemplation depend on the objects of your spirit's concentration and on whether your soul is looking at what's below, within, or above you.

63

*On the soul's powers, with a special look
at the mind as its major faculty, since the
mind comprehends all other strengths
and also their accomplishments*

The mind is such a miraculous power that any proper description of it must include this point: In a way, it really does no work. It comprehends and contains the powers of reason, will, imagination, and sensuality, as well as their works. But it can't be said to do any work itself, unless you consider this comprehension an activity.

I call some of the powers of the soul major and others minor—not because the soul can be split into parts, because obviously it can't, but its powers work with matters that can be analyzed into two categories: major or spiritual concerns and secondary or physical matters. Reason and will are the soul's two major active powers. They work solely by themselves to accomplish all spiritual advancements, with no help from the secondary powers. On the other hand, imagination and sensuality work through the body's five senses in the arena of the material, with things both present and absent, but they alone can't help us understand creation. We need reason and will to know the virtue and nature of other creatures and their reasons for being here and for doing what they do.

That's why reason and will are called major powers, because only they work in the sphere of the spiritual. Imagination and sensuality are considered secondary because their activity is confined to the body and its five senses. The mind is also regarded as a major power because it spiritually comprehends not only all of the other powers but also all of the objects on which they work. Let me show you.

64

---

*On the soul's two other special strengths,
reason and will, and their purpose
before sin and after*

Reason is the power that helps us distinguish the evil from the good, the bad from the worse, the good from the better, the worse from the worst, and the better from the best. Before humanity sinned, reason did all of this naturally, but now reason and original sin are so fused that reason cannot do the work of discernment unless grace illuminates its blindness. Reason and its object are comprehended and contained in the mind.

Will is the power that helps us choose the good that has been selected by reason. It also helps us love and desire this good and rest in God, completely confident and joyful. Before humanity knew sin, the will was never deceived. It decided, loved, and acted with integrity. The will experienced and appreciated the real worth of everything then. Now it can't, unless grace blesses its work. Infected by original sin, the will often delights in choosing something that only looks good, but is actually evil. The will and its object are contained and comprehended in the mind.

65

*A look at the work of imagination, the first
secondary power, and its obedience before
sin and disobedience after*

Imagination is the power that helps us form mental images of anything present or absent. Like reason and will, imagination and its work are contained in the mind. Before sin, imagination obeyed reason the way a good servant obeys its master—completely. Imagination never presented reason with perverted images of physical creatures or with spiritual illusions, but that's not true anymore. Unless imagination is restrained by the illumination of grace in our ability to reason, we're plagued night and day by unhealthy images of flesh-and-blood creatures and various fantasies, physical representations of spiritual realities or vice versa. These are always fake, fraudulent, and synonymous with error.

In the prayers of novices newly turned from the world to a life of devotion, this disobedience of the imagination surfaces. They are just starting out in this discipline and have not yet learned how to let reason's bright grace control their imagination. This self-mastery will naturally happen over time for those who keep reflecting on spiritual truths like their own human weaknesses, Christ's Passion, the kindness of our Lord God, and many other things, but until it does, they will be bombarded by various thoughts, fantasies, and images served up by their cunning imaginations and branded on their minds. And all of this disobedience is the painful aftermath of original sin.

66

---

*A look at the work of sensuality, the other
secondary power, and its obedience before
sin and disobedience after*

Sensuality is the power that affects and controls our body's perceptions. It allows us to know and experience all of physical creation, both pleasant and unpleasant. It works in two ways: it looks after our physical needs, and it also serves the pleasures of the five senses. This power complains when the body lacks what it needs, but it also makes us eat excessively and indulge our other appetites unhealthily. It gets annoyed when its friends are far away and is happy when they're present. It grumbles when it has to be with people it dislikes and rejoices when they're absent. It desires pleasure and tries to avoid discomfort of any kind. Like reason, will, and imagination, sensuality and its objects are contained in the mind.

Before sin, our sensuality was so obedient to the

will—as if it were its servant—that it never led the will down the wrong path. Unwholesome excess was never suggested, inordinate feelings of affection or dislike weren't possible, and all bogus spiritual experiences were unknown. For our spiritual enemy had no purchase on the soul then. But that's not true anymore. If grace doesn't rule the will, our sensuality never learns to suffer the consequences of original sin, because this submission requires humility. We must all learn to suffer well because each of us will experience the absence of pleasant things needed by the body and the presence of painful remorse, that unpleasant but beneficial godly sorrow that our spirits must embrace. We must also teach ourselves self-control for two reasons: so that we don't lust after the wonderful necessities of life and so that we don't rejoice too much in the absence of unpleasant but soul-nourishing godly sorrow. If we don't learn spiritual discipline in these areas, the power of sensuality will run wild. Like a pig in mud, it will wallow in filthy promiscuity and worldly possessions. At that point, a person's lifestyle is so beastly and carnal that they cease to be human or in any way spiritual.

67

*That ignorance of the soul's powers and
ways can make us misinterpret spiritual
instruction and contemplation, and how
grace transforms us, making us godly*

My dear friend in God, look at the misery caused by
original sin. Is it any wonder we are blind, easily deceived as we try to understand the vocabulary of the
spirit and the work of contemplation, especially if we
don't yet know the powers of our souls and how they
work?

When your mind is occupied with anything material,
no matter how worthwhile, remember that this physical
matter naturally ranks "below" you and that you are "outside" your spirit, but when your mind focuses on the
mysterious nature of your soul's faculties and on their
complex behavior, you grow in self-knowledge. This
introspection teaches you how each of the soul's powers strengthens virtues and heals vices in you and in

others on the same spiritual journey. During such self-reflection, you're "within" yourself and are "on the same level" as your potential. Eventually, this analysis of soul will teach you who you are. You mature along the path of purification. Best of all, when your mind is focused on nothing physical or spiritual, it's solely engaged with God's very essence. This is the work of contemplation, which this book teaches. You'll prove my words true when you practice this discipline and experience being "above" yourself and "under" your God.

When contemplation makes you one with God in spirit, love, and will, you're "above" yourself because you've only reached that state by grace and not by your own efforts. You're also "under" God then, even though contemplative prayer makes you one with God in spirit, no longer two. In this unity, which is the height of contemplation, you can be thought of as god-like, as Scripture says.[1] Still, you're below God because he's naturally eternal and you're not. God has no beginning, but there was a time when you didn't even exist. You were nothing, and after you were made by God's power and God's love, you willfully chose sin, making yourself worse than nothing. We deserve no mercy, but through his grace are made godly. Our souls are joined to him in spirit with no separation, both here and in heaven's joy, forever. This is how, though you're one with him in grace, you're still infinitely inferior to him in nature.

Do you see what I mean? My dear friend, you've learned, in part, how those ignorant of their souls' powers and activities can easily misinterpret words carrying a spiritual meaning. You also see why I did not dare recommend that you show your desire to God—I asked instead that you do everything possible to hide it from him and cover it up, like a child playing a game. I still recommend that because I worry you might physically construe what is meant spiritually.

68

*That nowhere physically is everywhere spiritually,
and how our visible, outer self calls the work
of this book "nothing"*

On a related point, another person might tell you to gather together your powers of body, soul, and intellect wholly within yourself, and worship God there. This is good advice, well put, and if taken in the right way, you can't find any better. But I don't recommend this because I worry that such advice might be literally interpreted and mislead someone. My suggestion resists distortion. I only ask that during contemplative prayer steer clear of withdrawing into yourself. I also don't want you outside, above, behind, or on one side or the other of yourself.

"Where then," you ask, "will I be? If I take your advice, I'll end up 'nowhere'!" You're right. Well said. That's exactly where I want you, because nowhere physically is everywhere spiritually. Make sure that your contemplative work is fully detached from the physical. Remember that when your mind is focused on anything in particular, that's where you are spiritually, just as certainly as when your physical being is located in a specific place, that's where your body is. Obviously during contemplative prayer, your body's five senses and your soul's powers will think that you are doing nothing because they find nothing to feed on, but don't let that stop you—keep on working at this "nothing," as long as you are doing it for God's love. Persevere in contemplation with a renewed longing in your will to have God, remembering that your intellect cannot possess him. For I would rather be nowhere physically, wrestling with this obscure nothing, than be a powerful, rich lord, able to go wherever I want, whenever I want, always amusing myself with every "something" that I own.

So abandon the world's "everywhere" and "something" in exchange for this infinitely more valuable nowhere and nothing. Don't be bothered that your intellect is unable to comprehend it. I love it even more for its inscrutability. Its infinite worth makes it incomprehensible. Also remember that you can more easily feel this nothing than see it. It can be experienced but not grasped. That's why it seems completely hidden and totally dark to those who've only been looking at it for a very short time. Let me clarify "dark" here.

When a person experiences this nothing, the soul is blinded by an abundance of spiritual light, and not by actual darkness or by an absence of physical light.

So who labels this "nothing"? That would be our outer self. Our inner self calls it "all," because experiencing this "nothing" gives us an intuitive sense of all creation, both physical and spiritual, without paying special attention to any one thing.

69

How a person's love is changed in wonderful ways during the spiritual experience of this nothing, happening nowhere

Experiencing this nothing in its nowhere miraculously transforms a person's soul, outlook, and capacity for love.[1] Contemplation totally changes a person's interior. Here's how. When the soul first begins looking at this nothing, what does it see? As if gazing on a dark, mysterious painting, it sees depicted there all its past sins, physical and spiritual, from day one on. No matter where the soul turns, these sins never leave its eyes, until after a period of much hard work, bitter remorse, and countless tears, the soul has virtually rubbed them all away.

At times during the agony[2] of this spiritual labor, the soul believes it's in hell. Looking at past sins is so horrible that it despairs of ever being healed or feeling at peace. Some only get this far. When the intense heartache is prolonged without their being comforted, they turn back to superficial concerns. Unable to face themselves, they look to the world for consolation, to fill their emptiness. If they had only endured a little longer, they would have found that this void was filled with spiritual comfort, but they lacked the patience to earn eternal consolation.

Those who wait on God in darkness are rewarded with comfort and hope. Their patience wins them glimpses of their spiritual growth, creating peace. They see many of their particular sins mostly rubbed away by grace and healed. This is the "perfection" that is the painful process of purification. Although our suffering continues, we gain a new, consoling confidence. We start believing that this pain will eventually end because already it grows less and less as time passes. So we begin to call this suffering not hell, but purgatory.

Sometimes when we look on this nothingness, we see no particular sin branded there, only the lump of sin itself, beyond analysis and yet also somehow who we are. This is original sin's root[3] and pain. Sometimes we think this nothingness is a heavenly paradise because it holds many different wonderful delights, comforts, joys, and strengths. Sometimes, too, we think it is God, because we discover peace and rest there.

Yes, think what you want of this nothingness. Regardless, you'll always find that it's a cloud of unknowing between you and God.

70

That where our five senses end, our spiritual experience begins, and where our spiritual understanding ends, we begin knowing God through grace, as best we can on earth

So, work diligently in this nothing, which is nowhere. Put aside your exterior ways of knowing, such as your five senses and their objects of interest, because I'm telling you that this contemplative work can't be accomplished by them.

Your eyes only understand that something is long, wide, small, large, round, square, near, far, and colorful. Your ears only comprehend noise or other sounds. Your nose only recognizes a stench or a fragrance. Taste only affords you the ability to know whether something is sour or sweet, salty or fresh, bitter or pleasant. And touch can only teach you whether something is hot or cold, hard or soft, or smooth or sharp. But God has none of these dimensions. In fact, nothing spiritual has these characteristics.

So stop trying to work with your body's senses in any way. Abandon them entirely. Those people who start the inner work of contemplation with the belief that they're supposed to hear, smell, see, taste, or touch spiritual things, inside or outside, are truly misled. They work against nature, taking the wrong approach. Although God has ordained that our body's senses should teach us about all external and physical things, I mean that in no way do the senses' various positive activities help us understand spiritual things. But we can learn much from their failures. Whenever we hear or read about something that our body's superficial senses cannot describe to us in any way, we can be sure that this thing is spiritual and not physical.

We have the same experience in contemplative work when we use our spiritual senses in our struggle to know God himself. Similar limitations apply. It doesn't matter how much profound wisdom we possess about created spiritual beings; our understanding cannot help us gain knowledge about any uncreated spiritual being, who is God alone. But the failure of our understanding can help us. When we reach the end of what we know, that's where we find God. That's why St. Dionysius said that the best, most divine knowledge of God is that which is known by not-knowing.

In fact, anyone who reads the books of Dionysius will find that his teaching clearly affirms everything that I have said so far or everything that I will say, from beginning to end. So I don't feel the need to cite him again to support what I'm teaching, nor do I need to quote from any other authority. In the past, writers followed the humble practice of not sharing their own opinions unless they supported their ideas with Scripture and with learned quotations from the Church Fathers, but now that practice has degenerated into arrogant erudition and clever grandstanding. You don't need that, so I won't do it. Instead, whoever has ears, let them hear,[1] and whoever is stirred to believe, let them. There's no other way.

71

---

*That some people only experience the
perfection of contemplation during
rare moments of ecstasy, while others
experience this whenever they want,
during each ordinary day*

Some people believe contemplation so difficult and so
awe-inspiring[1] that it can't be done without great struggle and that it's achieved only during those rare moments of ecstasy. I'll answer these people as best I can,
though my best will always be weak. Such matters depend entirely on God. Every person's individual spiritual journey will be different because as God carries
out his divine plan, he takes into consideration the
unique spiritual talents of each person to whom grace
has given the gift of contemplation and its practice.

It is true that some people can't reach the state of
contemplation without a long period of frequent practice, and even then they rarely experience the perfection of.this work, the God-given delight called ecstasy.

On the other hand, others are so wise in spirit and so at home with God in the grace of contemplation that they can feel this special ecstasy any time they want during the ordinary schedule of their day, while sitting, walking, standing, or kneeling. During these moments, they're in complete control of their physical and spiritual senses. They act normal. Internally they may experience this contemplative ecstasy as an interruption, but they remain calm without much difficulty. Moses is an example of the first type of contemplative, and Aaron, the priest of the temple, is an example of the second.[2]

In the Old Testament, the Ark of the Covenant symbolizes the grace of contemplation and, as the story illustrates, those who looked after the Ark then symbolize the contemplatives working in this grace today. The analogy of the Ark and contemplation is a good one because the Ark contained all of the jewels and relics of the temple, just as this little love focused on God in the cloud of unknowing contains all of the virtues of the soul, which is God's spiritual temple.[3]

Before Moses could see the Ark and receive its design, first he had to make that long, arduous climb up to the top of the mountain, where he stayed and worked in a cloud for six days. On the seventh day, our Lord gave him the design for the Ark.[4] Moses's prolonged effort and delayed vision symbolize those who can't reach the full height of this spiritual work without struggling a long time first and even then it only comes rarely, when God permits.

But what Moses found grueling and seldom received, Aaron already possessed. As a priest, Aaron had the power of his office and that allowed him to enter the temple and see the Ark behind the veil whenever he wanted. Aaron symbolizes those I described earlier, who by their spiritual skill and the help of grace can make the perfection of this work their own whenever they wish.

---

*That one contemplative's experience must
not be used to judge another's practice*

Surely you see from this that you shouldn't take your
own experience as the rule of thumb by which you
judge other contemplatives. For example, those who
must work really hard to reach the peak of contemplation, and then only get there occasionally, might make
the mistake of using their own experience as the standard for other contemplatives. We must remember
that not everyone has a difficult journey to the exceptional ecstasy. Some walk a simple path, routinely
meeting the miraculous in the ordinary. On the other
hand, these contemplatives must not make the opposite
assumption that their experience is universal. Not everyone feels the joy of contemplation whenever they
wish. Avoid both close-minded ways of thinking, for
you can't judge another's unique contemplative experience by your own. Besides, you can't know God's

wisdom; someone who has struggled a long time with prayer only to know the extraordinary transcendent moment may one day have these moments whenever they want and as often as they want. Moses is a good example of this. To start with, he only rarely caught a glimpse of the Ark's form and not without first working awfully hard on the mountain. But later, when the Ark was kept in the valley, Moses could see it as often as he liked.[1]

73

*That the Ark of the Covenant prefigures
contemplative grace, and Moses, Bezalel,
and Aaron and their dealings with the
Ark represent three contemplative ways*

Three men were the most involved with the Ark of the
Old Testament: they were Moses, Bezalel, and Aaron.
On the mountain, Moses learned (God taught him) how
to make the Ark.[1] In the valley, Bezalel used the design
Moses received on the mountain and created the Ark.[2]
And then in the temple, Aaron kept the Ark and tended
it there, seeing it and handling it as often as he liked.

These three men symbolize the three ways that we
advance in the grace of contemplation. Sometimes we
make progress by grace alone, and then we're most like
Moses, who for all of his climbing and hard work on
the mountain, only saw it seldom, and even then the
vision only came by our Lord's grace, when it pleased
God to reveal himself; it was not a reward for Moses's

diligent efforts. Sometimes we advance in contemplation by our own spiritual skill, helped[3] by grace, and then we're like Bezalel, who could not look on the Ark before he constructed it with his own skill, assisted by the blueprints given Moses on the mountain. And sometimes we advance in contemplation through the teaching of others, and then we're like Aaron, who was accustomed to seeing it and touching it whenever he wanted, but it was Bezalel who made the Ark and handed it to him.

So, spiritual friend, though my writing is as simple as a child's[4] and as awkward,[5] and though I'm certainly the worst teacher you can imagine, unworthy to instruct anyone, I bear the office of Bezalel, creating and making plain for you the nature of this spiritual Ark. Here, I put it in your hands. You can do far better than I, if you'll be Aaron. Dedicate yourself to gazing on the ark of contemplation without ceasing, for both of us. Do this, please, for the love of God Almighty. And since we are both called by God to do contemplative work, I ask you for the love of God, compensate (with your kind practice) for everything I lack.

74

---

*That when a soul is inclined to contemplation,
reading or hearing of it always resonates and
motivates, and a reprisal of the instructions
in the preface*

If you think this type of praying doesn't suit your temperament, abandon it and take another, with the help of wise counsel. Don't feel guilty about changing. If you do change, please don't blame me, since I only wanted to use my simple knowledge to help you advance in contemplation. That was my sole intent. So read it through two or three times, the more the better. Each time it will make more sense. Some section that was too hard for you to understand on a first or second reading will eventually seem easy.[1]

Yes, it seems impossible to me that anyone drawn by grace to contemplation could read or discuss this book privately or publicly without sensing an affinity with its message. So if this book seems to do you good, thank God with all your heart, and because you love him, pray for me.

So do the work. Also take me seriously when I ask you, for the love of God, don't share this book with anyone, unless you think they are equal to its contents. Remember what I said about this earlier. Read that chapter again where I describe what sort of person should start this exercise, and when. If you do allow another person to read this book, stress that they take their time and study it from cover to cover. I'm certain some topics discussed at the beginning or in the middle are left hanging without being fully explained, but these are clarified soon enough in the chapters that follow or at the very end of this book. A person who reads one section but not another might easily be led into error. So please do as I ask you.

Also, if you feel you need more information on any topic, just let me know which and tell me your thoughts about it, and I'll revise it as best I can, though my knowledge of such matters isn't much.

However, I really don't want habitual gossips, brown-nosers,[2] faultfinders, complainers, whisperers, and all kinds of character assassinators reading this book. I hope they never see it. I never intended to write anything for them. I don't even want them hearing about it. That also goes for those who are just inquisitive, both educated and not. Yes, I mean even if they are good people living active lives. It's not for the merely curious.

75

*On the signs that prove God is calling
a person to contemplation*

Many reading this book or hearing it read or discussed
will find it interesting, but not all of them are called by
God to do contemplative work. The pleasant emotion
some feel when reading it may come more from natural intellectual curiosity than from any calling of grace.

Here's how they can test the origin of this emotion
if they want. First let them see if they've done everything possible to prepare their conscience for this work.
By this I mean have they purified it, following the ob-
servances of the holy Church and the advice of their
spiritual director. When this is done, that much is
well.[1] If they want more confirmation, let them see if
the desire for contemplation presses on their minds at
all times, attracting their attention more than any other
spiritual discipline. Also, if their conscience can find
no peace in any physical or spiritual good they do, unless they make this secret little love-longing the primary

spiritual reason for everything they do, then it's proof that they are called by God to do this work. Otherwise, the answer is no.

I'm not saying that this stirring of love will be constant or permanent, even for those who are called to do this work. It just won't happen. Young spiritual apprentices starting out in contemplation often experience that the actual feeling is withdrawn from them for various reasons. Sometimes this happens so they won't take it for granted, assuming they control it and can have it whenever and however they like. Such a presumption would be pride. In fact, whenever the feeling of grace is withdrawn, arrogance is the explanation, not necessarily an actual, present pride but a latent pride that would emerge if this feeling of grace were never taken away. Often the young and foolish mistake its absence to mean that God is their enemy, when actually he's their best friend.[2] Sometimes this feeling is withdrawn because of their carelessness, and when that happens, the bitter pain of remorse soon overwhelms them.

Sometimes our Lord will delay it on purpose because he wants their waiting to make them appreciate this gift more. When that happens, it is one of the clearest, best signs that a soul has been called to do this spiritual work. Let's say you experience such a dry spell. If the gift comes back suddenly (as it does), independent of anything you've done, along with a larger desire and a stronger love-longing to do this work, so much so that your joy in finding it again is greater than the sorrow you had in losing it, then you know without a doubt God is calling you to do this work, no matter who you are or what you've done.

It is not who you are or what you've been that God sees with his merciful eyes, but what you want to be. St. Gregory says that "all holy desires grow when postponed, and the desire that diminishes with delay was never a holy desire." For example, those who feel less and less joy in new discoveries or in sudden encounters with old longings must know that even though these are natural desires for good things, they were never holy desires. St. Augustine teaches that "the whole life of a good Christian is nothing but holy desire."

Good-bye, dear friend. Go in God's blessing and mine. And I ask almighty God that true peace, wise[3] advice, divine joy, and abundant grace be with you always and with all on earth who love him. Amen.

NOTES

Introduction

1. Patrick J. Gallacher, ed., *The Cloud of Unknowing,* TEAMS Middle English Text Series (Kalamazoo, Mich.: Western Michigan University Medieval Institute Publications, 1997), 30, line 280.

2. Ibid., lines 284–85.

3. Ibid., lines 285–86.

4. Ibid., 31, line 288.

5. Ibid., lines 288–97. In the Old Testament, clouds are symbols of liberation and of God's love. Like the rock at Horeb (Exodus 17:6 and Isaiah 48:21), clouds showed the exiled Israelites that God never left them and would guide them every step of the long journey: Exodus 40:34–35, 13:21–22; Numbers 9:15–23; and Psalms 78:14. The cloud symbolizes God's loyalty to those stubborn ones he loves: Deuteronomy 1:31b–33; 1 Corinthians 10:1–4.

6. Gallacher, *The Cloud of Unknowing,* 31, line 290.

7. Matthew 22:37–39. The New Revised Standard Version (NRSV) of the Bible is used throughout. See Bruce M. Metzger, senior ed., *The New Revised Standard Version of the Bible (Anglicized Edition)* (New York: Division of Christian Education of the National Council of the Churches of Christ in the United States of America, 1995), www.devotions.net/bible/oobible.htm.

8. Gallacher, *The Cloud of Unknowing,* 36, lines 457–58.

9. Ibid., 35, lines 421–32.

10. Ibid., 37–38, lines 500–504.

11. Ibid., 31, lines 311–15.

12. Ibid., 68, lines 1451–53.

13. Ibid., 37, lines 497–98; 42, line 644; 55, line 1065; see also Phyllis Hodgson, ed., *The Cloud of Unknowing* and *The Book of Privy Counselling,* Early English Text Society Original Series Number 218 (London: Humphrey Milford, 1944), 135, line 20. For one of the best introductions ever written on these books, see Hodgson, *The Cloud of Unknowing* and *The Book of Privy Counselling,* ix-xc.

14. For more information, see Barbara Tuchman, *The Distant Mirror: The Calamitous Fourteenth Century* (New York: Ballantine Books, 1996), 93, and Philip Ziegler, *The Black Death* (New York: HarperCollins, 1971), 190.

15. John Kelly, *The Great Mortality: An Intimate History of the Black Death, the Most Devastating Plague of All Time* (New York: HarperCollins, 2005), 186, 277–78.

16. Tuchman, *The Distant Mirror,* 97.

17. The Boccaccio translation is my own. For the original Italian text and an early twentieth-century crib by J. M. Rigg, see Riva Massimo and Michael Papio, eds., Decameron Web, www.brown.edu/Departments/Italian_Studies/dweb/dweb.shtml.

18. Tuchman, *The Distant Mirror,* 373.

19. Dates for these writers are as follows: Richard Rolle died in 1349, Walter Hilton in 1396, Julian of Norwich in 1420, and the *Cloud*'s Anonymous in the late 1300s.

20. Here are dates for these medieval mystics: Birgitta died in 1373, Angela in 1309, Beatrijs in 1268, Catherine

of Siena in 1380, Meister Eckhart in 1328, Gertrude in 1302, Thomas à Kempis in 1471, Marguerite d'Oingt in 1310, Marguerite Porete in 1310, Mechthild of Hackeborn in 1298, Mechthild of Magdeburg in 1282, and Umiltà in 1310.

21. When Christian mystics talk of experiencing a "union with God," they are speaking of a spiritual journey. Bernard McGinn points out that the mystical element of the Christian religion is primarily a "way of life" rather than a "union with God" and that Christianity's mysticism is "that part of its beliefs and practices that concerns the preparation for, the consciousness of, and the reaction to the immediate or direct presence of God." See Bernard McGinn, *The Growth of Mysticism: Gregory the Great Through the 12th Century* (New York: Herder & Herder, 1996), x–xi.

22. See Bernard McGinn, ed., *The Essential Writings of Christian Mysticism* (New York: The Modern Library, 2006), 283–89 ("Dionysius: The Mystical Theology"); 155–71 ("Richard of St. Victor: The Four Degrees of Violent Charity," a shorter piece that had even more influence than his other works); and 27–34 ("Bernard of Clairvaux: Sermon on the Song of Songs 23"). *The Twelve Patriarchs* was also known as *The Preparation of the Soul for Contemplation.* To read *The Twelve Patriarchs,* see Grover A. Zinn, *Richard of St. Victor* (New York: Paulist Press, 1979), 51–147. The *Cloud* author's adaptation of Bernard of Clairvaux's sermons is found in his *Treatise of Discerning of Spirits.*

23. Hodgson, *The Cloud of Unknowing* and *The Book of Privy Counselling,* 152, lines 3–9.

24. Hodgson, *The Cloud of Unknowing* and *The Book of Privy Counselling,* xlix–l. Hodgson points out that the *Cloud*'s author was most likely from the north part of the central East Midlands.

25. Gallacher, *The Cloud of Unknowing,* 32–33, lines 347–56.

26. Ibid., 33, lines 357–65.

27. McGinn, *The Essential Writings of Christian Mysticism,* 283. Also see Ursula King, *Christian Mystics: Their Lives and Legacies throughout the Ages* (Mahwah, N.J.: HiddenSpring, 2001), 54–59. I prefer the shorter "Dionysius" over his longer moniker and also over the vernacular "Denys."

28. Whether Dionysius was more Neoplatonist or more Christian is often debated. The twentieth-century Eastern Orthodox theologian Vladimir Lossky argued that Dionysius is "a Christian thinker disguised as a Neoplatonist." For this quotation, see John Meyendorff, *Byzantine Theology: The Church and Social Reform* (New York: Fordham University Press, 1987), 27. Western mysticism scholar Bernard McGinn suggests that Dionysius "transposed pagan mystical philosophy in a way that would both give theological depth to Christian mystical traditions and also perhaps attract pagan thinkers to Christ." See McGinn, *The Essential Writings of Christian Mysticism,* 284.

29. This is my translation. For more information, see James Walsh, *The Cloud of Unknowing* (Ramsey, N.J.: Paulist Press, 1981), 48.

30. Bernard McGinn, *The Foundations of Mysticism: Origins to the Fifth Century,* Presence of God: A History of Western Christian Mysticism, vol. 1 (New York: Herder & Herder, 1994), 182.

31. McGinn, *The Essential Writings of Christian Mysticism,* 284.

32. Gallacher, *The Cloud of Unknowing,* 63, lines 1295–99.

33. Zinn, *Richard of St. Victor,* 1–2. Bernard McGinn and Patricia Ferris McGinn, *Early Christian Mystics: The Divine Vision of the Spiritual Masters* (New York: The Crossroad Publishing Company, 2003), 114–32.

34. Zinn, *Richard of St. Victor,* 23.

35. Ibid., 23–24. Thanks to Bill Rice, who read the manuscript in several of its early stages and whose astute marginalia included the Keats quotation, included here.

36. Bernard McGinn, *The Flowering of Mysticism: Men and Women in the New Mysticism*—1200–1350, Presence of God: A History of Western Christian Mysticism, vol. 3 (New York: Herder & Herder, 1998), 79–80.

37. Ibid., 82.

38. See Zinn, *Richard of St. Victor,* 55–60 (chapters 3–7 of *The Twelve Patriarchs*) and 155–58 (chapters 3 and 4 of *The Mystical Ark*).

39. See Exodus 25–27 and Cheryl Taylor, "Paradox upon Paradox: Using and Abusing Language in *The Cloud of Unknowing* and Related Texts," *Parergon* 22, no. 2 (July 2005): 38. Taylor's article is a brilliant analysis of this author's rhetorical style.

40. Gallacher, *The Cloud of Unknowing,* 99, lines 2444–49.

41. Kieran Kavanaugh, *John of the Cross: Selected Writings* (New York: Paulist Press, 1987), 62, 65. Augustine of Hippo is one of the most famous first mystics of the Western Christian tradition. For Augustine's descriptions of his own mystical experiences, see Henry Chadwick, trans., *St. Augustine Confessions* (Oxford: Oxford University Press, 1998). For Augustine's well-known

mystical conversation with his mother Monica, which took place at Ostia right before her death, see Chadwick, *St. Augustine Confessions,* 170ff.

42. J. M. Cohen, trans., *The Life of Saint Teresa of Avila by Herself* (New York: Penguin Classics, 1988), 85, 76, 125, 78, 101. See chapters 11–22, where Teresa discusses the four different ways to water the garden of the soul, each easier than the one before: the well (78ff), the windlass (98ff), the stream or spring (112ff), and the rain (122ff). Her dates are 1515–82.

43. Daniel Goleman, *Destructive Emotions: A Scientific Dialogue with the Dalai Lama* (New York: Bantam, 2003), 3–4.

44. Ibid., 3.

45. Gallacher, *The Cloud of Unknowing,* www.lib.rochester .edu/camelot/teams/cloud.htm and Frances McSparran, ed., *Middle English Dictionary,* http://quod.lib. umich.edu/m/med/. For help with the Middle English grammar, see chapter 6 of John Algeo, *Origins and Development of the English Language,* based on the original work of Thomas Pyles (New York: Cengage, 2009) and chapter 6 of John Algeo and Carmen Acevedo Butcher, *Problems in the Origins and Development of the English Language,* 7th ed. (New York: Cengage, 2014). For a splendid article on the *Cloud*'s contemplative *mimesis,* see Taylor, "Paradox upon Paradox."

Prayer for the Preface

1. The *Cloud* author uses the Middle English *entent* ("intent") often, reminding us that his theme is the exercise of "stretching" toward God. See Gallacher, *The Cloud of Unknowing,* 21, line 3. With his background in

Latin, he well knew that the word *entent* (our "intent") comes from the Latin *in,* "toward," and from *tendere,* "to stretch," so to be "intent" on something is literally "to stretch toward it." This anonymous monk shows us how we can stretch our minds toward God in contemplation and grow spiritually, becoming people who "make peace" (James 3:18). *Intense, tendon, attention, attend, attentive,* and *extend* share this Latin root "to stretch."

2. In Middle English, this prayer reads: *"God, unto Whom alle hertes ben open, and unto Whom alle wille spekith, and unto Whom no privé thing is hid: I beseche Thee so for to clense the entent of myn hert with the unspekable gift of Thi grace that I may parfiteliche love Thee, and worthilich preise Thee. Amen."* See Gallacher, *The Cloud of Unknowing,* 21, lines 2–5. Here we find a splendid example of the author's play on the words *speak* and *unspeakable,* highlighting that God listens to us when *alle wille* ("all longings") *spekith* ("speak") to him and that he answers our articulated or spoken longings with *the unspekable gift* ("the unspeakable gift") of his grace. We speak and in return are given an *unspekable* ("ineffable") gift, his grace. This wordplay deftly suggests the mystery of a dialogue between our chatter and a profound silence. This prayer is also the short opening prayer (or collect) before the epistle in the Roman Catholic votive Mass of the Holy Spirit (*Ad postulandam gratiam Spiritus Sancti*), with one difference: the anonymous author has slightly changed the original Latin version. Originally, the prayer addressed the unspeakable gift "of Your Holy Spirit," not "of Your grace." The author revised it to focus on God's grace. His use and revision of this liturgical prayer reveal his belief that

grace and the Holy Spirit are closely related, that the Holy Spirit informs contemplative prayer, that grace is the sine qua non of contemplation, and that communal prayer is central to spiritual growth.

Preface

1. If we picture the life of a medieval monastic community, this passage becomes clearer. Manuscripts (books) were precious. Monks wrote on vellum using styli, and production was time-intensive. Manuscripts were often read aloud in church, at chapter, and in the refectory. They were also read privately during the designated daily times of *lectio divina,* a slow, deliberate "sacred reading." The monastic librarian, or armarius, was responsible for "safekeeping" manuscripts for others. He looked after the armaria, closed cupboards in which manuscripts were stored, and he often did double duty as the leader of the choir (the precentor or cantor), because the service books were his main responsibility. The armarius also examined the manuscripts regularly, looking for mold, bookworms, or damage, and he was responsible for giving them out to the scriptorium for transcription and for loaning them to other monastic libraries.

2. In Middle English, "the active life" (*in actyve levyng*) is a complex concept, which the anonymous author fully describes in chapter 8. Here in the preface (see Gallacher, *The Cloud of Unknowing,* 21, lines 14–15), he seems to be dialoging with someone who has already taken a monastic vow. The author understands that those living "the active life" will be wholly focused on God in doing good deeds and in making moral decisions. He

believes that they will also be serious about advancing in prayer and about cultivating inner virtues.

3. Monks are famous for worrying that others will be led astray by their writings. The *Cloud* author uses "error" (*errour*) here not only to mean "misunderstanding," but also to indicate a flawed way of thinking that would take the reader off the path of grace and into damnation. See Gallacher, *The Cloud of Unknowing*, 22, line 26. Because he feels responsible for others' souls, he even tells them how to read his book—in its entirety. The tenth-century English Benedictine abbot, Ælfric of Eynsham, voices a similar concern when he instructs future scribes to copy down his sermons carefully so that they do not accidentally alter their salvation-bringing message. As Ælfric before him, the anonymous author of the *Cloud* is charged with the responsibility of being a spiritual director for others' souls. Therefore, he warns them (and us) to read his book with the diligence of the *lectio divina,* slowly, meditatively, steeping in the words.

4. This list of immaturities defines who the *Cloud*'s audience is not. The passage is worth reading in Middle English for the alliteration, rhythm, arresting diction, and brisk tone that make it crackle: *Fleschely janglers, opyn preisers and blamers of hemself or of any other, tithing tellers, rouners and tutilers of tales, and alle maner of pinchers, kept I never that thei sawe this book.* See Gallacher, *The Cloud of Unknowing,* 22, lines 28–30. This catalog of errors is also an allusion to the New Testament book of James and its description of the human tongue and need for discipline: "How great a forest is set ablaze by a small fire! And the tongue is a fire. The tongue is placed among

our members as a world of iniquity; it stains the whole body, sets on fire the cycle of nature and is itself set on fire by hell. For every species of beast and bird, of reptile and sea creature, can be tamed and has been tamed by the human species, but no one can tame the tongue—a restless evil, full of deadly poison. With it we bless the Lord and Father, and with it we curse those who are made in the likeness of God. From the same mouth come blessing and cursing. My brothers and sisters, this ought not to be so" (James 3:5b–10).

5. In Middle English, this phrase reads: *corious lettred or lewed men* (literally, "curious lettered or lay men"). See Gallacher, *The Cloud of Unknowing,* 22, lines 31–32. My translation stresses that, above all, the anonymous monk author frowns on anyone's idle curiosity, no matter who you are. He discourages the sport of spiritual specula- tion, where thinking for the sake of thinking eclipses the desire to know and serve God better. His *lettred* ("lettered, educated") refers to the religious clergy of his day. They were the sole educated members of society (outside of royalty and the few other wealthy people). *Lewed men* literally means "laymen," and by association, the "uneducated." The word *lewd* has since degenerated to signify something that is obscene.

Chapter 1

1. The Middle English here is *parfite,* literally "perfect." See Gallacher, *The Cloud of Unknowing,* 28, line 226. I went with the original. However, the word *pure* might work better, because *perfect* has such rigid, negative con- notations in the postmodern world. The *Cloud*'s thesis

is that the practice of contemplation *purifies* our hearts. We often misunderstand *perfect* to mean, "never making a mistake," but the anonymous monk is not describing a state of flawlessness. He wants us to participate in a spiritual experience that is an ongoing process of spiritual purification. As such, this process has more in common with the etymology of *perfect* than with its unyielding denotations. The Latin *perficio* ("perfect") breaks down into the root, *fácere* ("to do"), and the prefix, *per* ("through" or "thoroughly"). It means, "thoroughly or conscientiously do" something. In medieval literature, *parfite* ("perfect") points to a "refined" or "pure" soul or heart. Christianity has a long tradition of viewing salvation as an ongoing spiritual transformation. Gregory of Nyssa compares this "perfecting" to the process of refining gold, as he writes in his *Life of Macrina*: "Just as gold is heated in many furnaces, one after another, so any impurity not separated in the first furnace can be separated in the second, and so on, until any final impurity is removed in the last smelting. Macrina's good heart was refined . . . until it was absolutely pure."

2. According to an early Latin translator named Richard Methley, the *ordinary* degree refers to laypeople, the *special* degree to clerics or monastics, and the *singular* degree to solitaries such as hermits, anchorites, and Carthusians, for it was not usual then for a monk to leave an approved religious order for a hermitage, unless he were a Carthusian monk. See James Walsh, *The Cloud of Unknowing* (Ramsey, N.J.: Paulist Press, 1981), 116, footnote 14. From this logic, Methley suggests and Walsh agrees that the *Cloud* was written for a

Carthusian monk (9), but Evelyn Underhill disagrees, arguing that "the rule of that austere order, whose members live in hermit-like seclusion and scarcely meet except for the purpose of divine worship, can hardly have afforded him opportunity of observing and enduring all those tiresome tricks and absurd mannerisms of which he gives so amusing and realistic a description in the lighter passages of the *Cloud*." See her 1942 edition of *The Cloud of Unknowing* (New York: Cosimo Classics, 2007), 4–5. In "Paradox upon Paradox," Cheryl Taylor also assumes that the author "probably moved" in "Carthusian circles" (33). Anyone who has read Nancy Klein Maguire's cultural history of this order, *An Infinity of Little Hours* (New York: Public Affairs, 2006), has met several unforgettable Carthusian brothers and can easily imagine the *Cloud* author as a Carthusian. For example, we hear the medieval *Cloud* author's theme voiced hundreds of years later by the more recent Carthusian Dom Columba, who explains that when he rereads Teresa of Avila's *Interior Castle,* he always stops to pray: "Because she makes you see that God loves you—the whole point of Carthusian life" (238).

3. Walsh notes that an early commentator cites Christ as having lived through these four stages. When Christ was subject to his parents, he was in the ordinary degree; when he was preaching and healing, he was in the special degree; when he was fasting in the desert and praying on the mountain, he was in the singular degree; and when he experienced the transfiguration, resurrection, and ascension, he was in the perfect degree. See Walsh, *The Cloud of Unknowing,* 116.

4. This "leash of longing" is literally a "leash" in the original text (*lyame*), a *lyame of longing*. See Gallacher, *The Cloud of Unknowing,* 29, line 238. The word *lyame* made medieval readers picture leashes used to keep hounds from starting the chase too early when hunting boar or deer. Medieval readers also knew the short leather leashes called "jesses" were used by falconers for training female falcons to hunt other birds. Not unlike the gradual process of discipleship, training a falcon requires much patience from the falconer. He starts by tying the leash to one of the bird's legs and letting it fly short distances, until finally it can be loosed to fly free and far and trusted to return to its master. Through this simple, common image of restraint, the *Cloud*'s author powerfully communicates the complex, abstract concept of growing spiritually.

5. Literally, this phrase is "so that you could be a servant of his special servants" (*a servaunt of the special servauntes of His*). See Gallacher, *The Cloud of Unknowing,* 29, line 239. Walsh believes that "special servants" refers to the Carthusian monks in the community where the disciple is living because the twelfth-century Carthusian prior Hugo de Balma discusses what "specially chosen" means for the Carthusian vocation: "[Jesus] has called [the Carthusian disciple] not to the rule of the holy Benedict or Augustine . . . but has chosen him for that most blessed life which [Jesus] himself chose when he was led into the desert. He was our forerunner, showing what it means to be a servant, by serving us." See Walsh, *The Cloud of Unknowing,* 116–17, footnote 17. If the anonymous monk-author was not a Carthusian, he may simply mean

that all monastics have a "special" calling. In translating this passage, I retained its literal, specialized meaning while giving it a more inclusive tone.

6. This word *pulled* is exactly the same word in Middle English; it means "moved or dragged." In the Middle Ages, *pulled* also meant (as it does today) "picked ripe berries and fruits." The metaphor of organic growth and spiritual maturation runs through the *Cloud,* and the rich connotations of *pulled* are important to consider. See Gallacher, *The Cloud of Unknowing,* 29, line 244.

7. This "you'll learn to lift up the foot of your love" literally reads *thou maist lerne to lift up the fote of thi love.* See Gallacher, *The Cloud of Unknowing,* 29, lines 245–46. This foot of love is an Augustinian metaphor from his commentary on Psalm 9, where he says that love is "the foot of the soul." See Walsh, *The Cloud of Unknowing,* 117, footnote 18.

Chapter 2

1. The Middle English verb *lōken* ("lock") has two distinct meanings, and the anonymous author is aware of both here: (1) "to lock a door or an entrance, to secure a gate," and (2) "to look on, gaze at, stare." He wants us to "lock" our "gaze" on God, or, as the popular song says, "I only have eyes for you." See Gallacher, *The Cloud of Unknowing,* 30, lines 267–68.

2. This ancient Christian metaphor compares the five senses to "openings" through which bad influences can seduce the soul. See Gallacher, *The Cloud of Unknowing,* 30, lines 268–69. In the medieval *Scale of Perfection,* Walter Hilton writes: "Sin comes into your soul through five windows.

As Jeremiah said, 'Death has come up into our windows' (9:21). These 'windows' are the five senses through which your soul exits to pursue perverse pleasures and to feed on earthly things, contrary to the dignity of our natures. . . . So board up these windows. Only open them when you absolutely need to." This translation is my own. See also John P. H. Clark and Rosemary Dorward, trans., *Walter Hilton: The Scale of Perfection* (New York: Paulist Press, 1990), 149–50.

Chapter 3

1. As found in the *Book of Common Prayer,* this prayer is called the *sursum corda* and is included in the liturgy for the Holy Eucharist. The anonymous monk revisits this theme in chapter 58. See Gallacher, *The Cloud of Unknowing*, 30, line 274.

2. "Stirring" here is literally *steryng* in Middle English. It is one of the author's favorite words. See Gallacher, *The Cloud of Unknowing*, 30, line 274.

3. "Reaching" here is literally *streche* ("stretching"). Like the etymology of the word *entent* ("intent"), this notion of "stretching" our souls to God shows the author's debt to fifth-century teachings on contemplation, particularly those by Dionysius. See Gallacher, *The Cloud of Unknowing*, 30, line 278.

4. Throughout, the anonymous monk simply calls contemplation *werk* ("work"), which I sometimes translate as "exercise." See Gallacher, *The Cloud of Unknowing*, 30, line 280. He chooses such a common word because he wants us to know that contemplation is basic to our lives, the way the "work" of washing dishes is, too. Also,

in this word *werk,* he would have had in mind the *Opus Dei,* or "work of God," the daily monastic liturgical singing of Psalms.

5. Literally, *a cloude of unknowyng.* See Gallacher, *The Cloud of Unknowing,* 31, line 289. The contemplative concepts of "darkness" and "unknowing" are found in *The Mystical Theology* by Dionysius. See Bernard McGinn, *The Essential Writings of Christian Mysticism* (New York: The Modern Library, 2006), 283–89 ("Dionysius: The Mystical Theology").

6. "You'll only know that in your will you feel a simple reaching out to God," is *thou felist in thi wille a nakid entent unto God.* (Literally, "You'll feel in your will a naked intent toward God.") See Gallacher, *The Cloud of Unknowing,* 31, line 290. As with "stirring," mentioned above in footnote 2, "naked intent" is one of the author's favorite phrases.

Chapter 4

1. "So you won't go down the wrong path in this work" is *But forthi that thou schalt not erre in this worching.* (Literally, "But so that you shall not err in this work.") See Gallacher, *The Cloud of Unknowing,* 31, line 299. The Middle English verb *erren* ("to err") has several levels of meaning. The obvious one is "to wander, to deviate, to sin, to make a mistake." It can also mean "to make a person angry," the overtones of which may be intended here: "So you won't go down the wrong path, fall into sin, and become angry." As a noun, *erre* can mean "scar or wound," as well as "anger," and *errer* is also Middle English for "heretic." So the anonymous monk is saying

more than, "So you won't make a mistake." He wants to prevent his disciple from getting any wrong ideas that would scar his soul for life and for eternity. He also wants his disciple's anger purified into spiritual peace.

2. The fifth-century-B.C. Greeks Leucippus of Miletus and his student Democritus of Abdera developed the concept of the atom. Democritus coined the term, ἄτομος or *átomos,* meaning "indivisible" or "uncuttable." It originally denoted a particle that cannot be cut into smaller particles. Here it retains their meaning of "the smallest particle." Today the atom has been replaced by the world of subatomic particles. The medieval person understood an *attōme* or the *athomus* to be the smallest unit of time. And 22,560 "atoms" were thought to be in each hour, which made one atom represent one 15/94th of a second. A century after Leucippus and Democritus, Epicurus and Lucretius refined the logic of atomic theory and, with only minor changes, this theory lasted the next two thousand years. See Bernard Pullman's *The Atom in the History of Human Thought* (New York: Oxford University Press, 2001), 31–47.

3. Julian of Norwich also discusses the "littleness" of this world, as she says in her *Revelations:* "In my vision I saw something small. No bigger than a hazelnut, it lay in the palm of my hand, round as a ball. Looking at it with the eye of my understanding, I wondered, 'What is that?' I was given to understand it is everything in creation. That this minute thing lasted at all amazed me. It was so tiny, it looked as if it would suddenly vanish into nothing. Concerning this tiny, hazelnut-sized cosmos, I received this answer in my soul, 'It lasts and always will

because God loves it.' I saw then that everything's alive through God's love." See Carmen Acevedo Butcher, *A Little Daily Wisdom* (Brewster, Mass.: Paraclete Press, 2008), 159.

In *The Atom in the History of Human Thought* (on the epigraph page), Pullman quotes physicist Richard P. Feynman on "little particles": "If all scientific knowledge were lost in a cataclysm, what single statement would preserve the most information for the next generations of creatures? How could we best pass on our understanding of the world? [I might propose:] 'All things are made of atoms—little particles that move around in perpetual motion, attracting each other when they are a little distance apart, but repelling upon being squeezed into one another.' In that one sentence, you will see, there is an enormous amount of information about the world, if just a little imagination and thinking are applied."

4. A medieval reader would have reflected here on the Parable of the Talents in the gospel of Matthew and on how the servants in this story were required to give an account to their master of how they spent the money that he had given them to invest. To the one who had dug a hole and hid his money selfishly and uselessly in the ground, the master said: "So take the talent from him and give it to the one with the ten talents. For to all those who have, more will be given, and they will have an abundance; but from those who have nothing, even what they have will be taken away" (Matthew 25:28–29).

5. Cf. Ephesians 3:18–20: "I pray that you may have the power to comprehend, with all the saints, what is the

breadth and length and height and depth, and to know the love of Christ that surpasses knowledge, so that you may be filled with all the fullness of God. Now to him who by the power at work within us is able to accomplish abundantly far more than all we can ask or imagine, to him be glory in the church and in Christ Jesus to all generations, for ever and ever."

6. Cf. Mark 2:27: "Then Jesus said, 'The sabbath was made for humankind, and not humankind for the sabbath.'"

7. In scholastic thought, angels do not experience time. They are spirits only, without physicality and without motion, and time cannot exist without these two qualities, so angels were seen as existing outside time. Instead, angels were said to live in the *aévum*, that indivisible locale between eternity and time.

8. The "sudden impulse" flying up to God "like a spark from a burning coal" is a typical Dionysian simile.

Chapter 5

1. This "live and work" is an alliterative phrase in Middle English: *wone and worche.* See Gallacher, *The Cloud of Unknowing*, 35, line 421. "Live" is *wone,* from the infinitive, *wonen* ("to live"), and *wonen* has two distinct meanings: first, "to live or to stay somewhere," and second, "to moan or to lament." The second definition would have flickered across a medieval reader's mind, as a reminder of the humility and godly sorrow required by true contemplation.

Chapter 6

1. The Middle English diction in this section has deliberate military overtones. Real physical conflict is never

intended, but spiritual warfare is. The *Cloud* author writes here, "Even meditating on God's love must be *put down*." See Gallacher, *The Cloud of Unknowing*, 36, line 461. This sentence features the Middle English verb-and-preposition combination for "put down," which is *casten down,* but *casten down* can also mean "to hurl missiles with a siege engine," "to fire stones or throw fire," "to shoot an arrow," or "to throw down in wrestling." It also means "to throw away," "to reject," and "to neglect," a reminder of Jesus's strong words in the Gospel of Matthew: "And everyone who has left houses or brothers or sisters or father or mother or children or fields, for my name's sake, will receive a hundredfold, and will inherit eternal life" (19:29). The next phrase, "and covered with a cloud of forgetting," uses the verb *keverid* ("covered"), creating an image in the mind of a soldier "covering" a dead body on a battlefield. Later in the same paragraph, in "beat on that thick cloud of unknowing with the sharp arrow of longing," the "beat" is *smyte* (literally, "smite"), which can also mean "to do battle with," "to slash with a sword," or "to strike with an arrow." The "sharp arrow" is *scharp darte* (literally "sharp dart") and can also mean "a metal-pointed missile, such as a javelin or spear, hurled by hand." The military imagery here is very like that found in the equally anonymous Anglo-Saxon poem, "The Dream of the Rood," where the personified Cross describes Christ as an eager warrior who runs naked to the Cross and leaps onto it willingly, bravely, and without hesitation. Perhaps the anonymous author of the *Cloud* knew this earlier Christocentric classic. See my translation of "The Dream of the Rood" at www.carmenbutcher.com.

Chapter 7

1. "Sit down" here is *go doun* (literally "go down"). See Gallacher, *The Cloud of Unknowing*, 37, line 472. *Go doun* is a common medieval verb-and-preposition combination used for actions like sitting down at the supper table; also, a misbehaving child might be told to *go doun* ("sit down"). This phrase can also mean "to fall down, kneel, or prostrate oneself." In other words, the author commands his unruly thoughts to bow before God and get quiet, as a child should do before his or her father.

2. "Dismiss" is actually more forceful and more physical in Middle English; it is the verb, *treed*. See Gallacher, *The Cloud of Unknowing*, 37, line 472. "Dismiss these thoughts" is *Treed him,* literally meaning "tread on it" or "trample on it" or "stomp on it." The author uses the pronoun *him* here for "thought" instead of *it* because he is personifying each thought. The *Cloud* author's diction here closely associates our thoughts with the devil and his tempting. I have chosen to use *these* and *it* throughout, instead of *him,* to avoid confusion and awkwardness for the postmodern reader. In short, the author wants the contemplative to "stomp" on thoughts as they arise, as if crushing the devil.

3. The Middle English here is the masculine pronoun *he* ("he"), not my translated *it,* another example of how the author is personifying a person's thought. See Gallacher, *The Cloud of Unknowing*, 37, line 473.

4. "It will be your shield and spear, whether you ride out into peace or conflict" is *This word schal be thi scheeld and thi spere, whether thou ridest on pees or on were.* (Literally, "This word shall be your shield and your spear, whether you ride out into peace or war.") See Gallacher, *The Cloud of Unknowing*, 38, lines 505–6. This is another instance of a military metaphor used to indicate spiritual warfare and the ways that the discipline of contemplation strengthens those grappling with their unruly selves.

Chapter 8

1. "I'll try to answer them as best I can" is *I think to answere therto so febeli as I can.* (Literally, "I think to answer them as feebly as I can.") See Gallacher, *The Cloud of Unknowing*, 38, lines 525–26. This humility, while extreme to the postmodern mind, is a traditional (and heartfelt) characteristic of any medieval religious teacher.

2. The author's use of "lower" and "higher" throughout his letters to his disciple conjures up the implied and very traditional image of the ladder of humility. Benedict of Nursia outlines in his monastic *Rule* the twelve steps of this ladder, and he explains that its template is "the ladder of Jacob, on which God's angels were seen going up and down between heaven and earth, [which] symbolizes the dialogue each one of us needs with God." The Desert Mother Amma Sarah also says, "Before starting up the ladder of humility, I fix my eyes on death."

3. This sentence alludes to the Gospel of Luke: "But the Lord answered her, 'Martha, Martha, you are worried and distracted by many things; there is need of only one

thing. Mary has chosen the best part, which will not be taken away from her'" (10:41–43). The New Revised Standard Version (NRSV) of the Bible has "the better part" for "the best part," but to keep the NRSV Bible verses consistent with the Middle English text, which has *the best partye,* I have inserted "best" for "better" in the NRSV verses, too.

4. In an e-mail message from September 3, 2007, the American West scholar Bill Rice describes the challenge that we all face of finding peace in a world where "there are always problems": "Joan Didion's line always comes back to me. Riffing on the old cowboy and Indian myth in her essay called 'On Self Respect' (from *Slouching Toward Bethlehem*), she says, 'Indians were simply part of the donnée,' meaning of course that something is always there to threaten your sanity, wreck your plans, or be petty. But I continue to believe with MLK, Jr. that the universe tends toward truth—even in small things."

5. This phrase, "is only darkness" (*hongeth al holy in this derknes*), literally is "hangs all wholly in darkness," but *hongeth* can also be used for a prisoner's "hanging" in crucifixion, a deliberate reminder of Christ's Passion. The *holy* ("wholly" or "entirely") is an effective pun for the modern "holy" or "sacred." The author's diction here cleverly suggests that the "darkness" of the second stage of contemplation is synonymous with *holy* Christ's *radiant* and *wholly* sacrificial love. See Gallacher, *The Cloud of Unknowing,* 39, lines 564–65.

6. These "loving nudges" are *lovyng steryng* (literally, "loving stirring"). See Gallacher, *The Cloud of Unknowing,* 39, line 565. The author is fond of *steryng* and uses it often.

Steryng connotes love's tenderness and is a perfect foil, even an antidote, for the author's many instances of violent military metaphors depicting the equally necessary spiritual warfare of the diligent soul.

Chapter 9

1. This "secret" is *privé* in Middle English. See Gallacher, *The Cloud of Unknowing*, 41, line 605. It is also found in the title of the sequel to the *Cloud, The Book of Privy Counsel*. There and here *privy* means many things: "hidden, personal, private, intimate, confidential, peculiar, special, mystic, unseen, invisible, internal, imperceptible, and unknown." This "*secret* love beats" on the cloud of unknowing, and in Middle English, "beats" is the word, *put,* for "thrusts." It's what knights do in battle: *In his sadle he held him still And smote Darel with so goode will, In middes of the sheld ful butt, That Darel fell doun with that putt* ("In his saddle he held himself still and then hit Darel with all his might in the middle of his shield, and Darel fell down with that *blow* [author's emphasis].") This example from 1450 A.D. is found in the University of Michigan online Middle English dictionary; see *A Royal Historie of the Excellent Knight Generides,* edited by F. J. Furnivall (line 4588).

Chapter 10

1. The medieval Roman Catholic Church also divided sin into the two categories of mortal and venial. Mortal (also "capital" or "deadly") sins threatened the soul with eternal damnation and had to be absolved through the sacrament of confession and genuine godly sorrow.

Venial sins were considered less serious and more easily forgiven. *Venial* originates in the Latin *veniábilis,* for "pardonable," and the word is associated with love because it is linked etymologically with *Venus,* the Roman goddess of beauty and love. There's also a connection with "sexual love" (compare the etymology of *venereal*).

2. These are the traditional seven deadly sins. For an identical list contemporary with this one from the *Cloud,* see Chaucer's "Parson's Tale." Over the years, these seven deadly sins have remained consistent, with only minor changes. In the sermon, *Dominica III in Quadragesima* ("For the Third Sunday in Lent"), by the tenth-century English Benedictine monk, Ælfric, eight deadly sins are listed, including melancholy and narcissism, but not envy. See John C. Pope's *Homilies of Ælfric: A Supplementary Collection* (London: Oxford University Press, 1967, 1968), vol. 1, sermon IV, lines 249–51, and for a modern translation of this Old English sermon with its list of deadly sins, see Carmen Acevedo Butcher's *God of Mercy: Ælfric's Sermons and Theology* (Macon, Ga.: Mercer University Press, 2006), 59. Bede listed seven deadly sins but did not name them; Haymo also listed seven, putting pride (*superbia*) first, as the worst. For lists of sins in the Bible, see Proverbs 6:16–19, Galatians 5:19–21, and 1 Corinthians 6:6–10.

Chapter 12

1. In Middle English, the title of this chapter, "How contemplation destroys sin and nurtures virtues," is a splendid example of the author's penchant for wordplay. Literally it reads, *That by vertewe of this werk sinne is*

not only distroied, bot also vertewes ben getyn ("That by the power of this work sin is not only destroyed, but also virtues are gained"). The first *vertewe* means "power," and the second *vertewe* means "virtue" in the sense of "moral excellence." See Gallacher, *The Cloud of Unknowing*, 23, lines 66–67. This pun brings out the true meaning of *virtue,* which is "power," and since the etymology of this word is *vir* for "man," the author is likely thinking about the man who redeemed the world—Christ— whose "power" makes the virtues possible, as seen in Hildegard of Bingen's twelfth-century play, *Ordo virtutum*. In this liturgical play, Hildegard personifies the virtues as women who fight and defeat the devil. They are Knowledge-of-God, Queen Humility, Charity, Respect for the Awe-Inspiring God, Obedience, Faith, Hope, Chastity, Innocence, Contempt-for-the-World, Divine Love, Discipline, Modesty, Compassion, Victory, Discernment, and Patience. Of course, these virtues are the antidotes to the seven deadly sins.

2. This phrase is literally, *schere awei thi prevé membres* ("do away with [or chop off] the private members"). See Gallacher, *The Cloud of Unknowing*, 44, line 688.

3. See Luke 10:42.

4. "Mature" here is *ordeinde* ("ordered"), from *ordeinen* ("to order"). See Gallacher, *The Cloud of Unknowing*, 44, line 702. The medieval mind always associates "virtues" with "order." See the title and theme of Hildegard of Bingen's musical, *Ordo virtutum* ("Order of the Virtues"). Some of the definitions of *ordeinen* are "to organize," "to prepare," "to regulate, control, or govern," "to subordinate (one's will to God's will)," "to arrange (troops in battle

formation)," and "to station (guards or watchmen)." The medieval use of "order" often connotes spiritual battles, as it does here, even in the adjectival past participle form of the verb.

Chapter 13

1. "Words fail me" is literally, *I defaile to sey what schuld falle of hem* ("I fail in trying to say what should befall them [these people]"). See Gallacher, *The Cloud of Unknowing*, 45, lines 724–25. This *defaile* sums up what our author thinks of language; it can only take us so far in getting to know God. Eventually, we come to the end of words and thinking, and that is when we begin to touch God. The *hem* ("them") refers not only to people, but also to saints and angels.

Chapter 15

1. The "sins we have committed in the past" is literally *oure before-done synnes* ("our before-done sins"), an original linguistic construct emphasizing not just that the sins happened in the past, but that they happened "before" *and* were "done" by us. In other words, we had a choice, and we chose to do them. "Before-done sins" is a splendid representation of the psychological state leading to guilt, or to godly sorrow—through a focus on ignoble, "before-done" actions. See Gallacher, *The Cloud of Unknowing*, 46, line 774.

2. In "until the *awful* rust of sin is scrubbed away in an *awesome* manner," the "awful" and "awesome" are my attempt to duplicate the author's splendid wordplay. He plays on the word "great" (*grete*) in the original,

when he writes, *the grete rust of oure sinne be in grete party rubbid awey* ("the great rust of our sin will be in great part rubbed away"). See Gallacher, *The Cloud of Unknowing*, 46, lines 777–78.

3. The reference is to the Sermon on the Mount: "Be perfect, therefore, as your heavenly Father is perfect" (Matthew 5:48).

Chapter 16

1. This Gospel story is found in Luke 7:36–50. See this passage: "Then turning toward the woman, Jesus said to Simon, 'Do you see this woman? I entered your house; you gave me no water for my feet, but she has bathed my feet with her tears and dried them with her hair. You gave me no kiss, but from the time I came in she has not stopped kissing my feet. You did not anoint my head with oil, but she has anointed my feet with ointment. Therefore, I tell you, her sins, which were many, have been forgiven; hence she has shown great love. But the one to whom little is forgiven, loves little.' Then he said to her, 'Your sins are forgiven'" (Luke 7:44–48).

2. This passage is rich with imagistic connotations: "Although she [Mary] could never undo the deep, heartfelt regret for her sins—they accompanied her wherever she went, a burden wrapped up and secretly hidden in the hole of her heart, not forgotten." In Middle English, it reads: *Scho, thof al scho myght not unfele the depe hertly sorow of hir synnes—for whi al hir liiftyme sche had hem with hir whereso sche gede, as it were in a birthen bounden togeders and leide up ful prively in the hole of hir herte, in maner*

never to be forgeten. See Gallacher, *The Cloud of Unknowing*, 47, lines 814–17. This description of Mary's sins looks ahead to chapter 36 and its reference to sin as a "lump." Her godly sorrow for her sins is called her "burden" (*birthen*), which in Middle English can also mean "something carried within the body or as part of the body; a fetus"; it can also mean "the bearing of a child in the womb, gestation." In other words, Mary's grieving for her sins (*birthen*) will "birth" (*birthen*) her soul into a closer relationship with God. *Hole* in Middle English can also mean "a cavern, cave, cleft in the rock; a pit," and is suggestive of a womb.

3. "Heartfelt" here is *hertly,* creating resonant wordplay with the earlier *in the hole of hir* herte ("in the hole of her *heart*"). Because of the "burden" of godly sorrow lodged deep in Mary Magdalene's heart, she knew *hertly sorow* (literally, "heartfelt sorrow"). See Gallacher, *The Cloud of Unknowing*, 47, lines 816–17; 47–48, lines 814–18.

4. In Middle English, this "sadder" is *more doelful* (our modern "doleful," in "more doleful"). See Gallacher, *The Cloud of Unknowing*, 48, line 818. *Doelful* means "full of sorrow, sad, grief-stricken." It rhymes with the earlier *hole [of hir herte],* placing aural emphasis on the fact that this *hole* is *doelful,* the secret hurt of every heart, giving new meaning to "heartfelt sorrow."

5. William Johnston glosses this *donghille* ("dunghill") as "cesspool," which works nicely, but I kept the original because it speaks to the traditional Christian image of a person's sitting on a dunghill when defeated. See 1 Samuel 2:8, Psalms 113:7, and Lamentations 4:5. See Gallacher, *The Cloud of Unknowing*, 48, line 828.

6. "Hung" here is *heng,"* from *hōngen,* which can also mean "to hang on a Cross." See Gallacher, *The Cloud of Unknowing,* 48, line 834. So this verb carries with it the suggestion that Mary is letting her own will be crucified with Christ on the cross. We can make a modern example of wordplay by saying that she "hung up" her "hang-ups" in God's sacrificial love.

7. See Luke 10:38–42.

Chapter 17

1. Luke 10:39.

2. The translation tries to capture the author's clever and emphatic wordplay: *Ther was never yit pure creature in this liif, ne never yit schal be, so highe ravischid in contemplacion and love of the Godheed, that ther ne is evermore a highe and a wonderful cloude of unknowyng bitwix him and his God.* See Gallacher, *The Cloud of Unknowing,* 49, lines 856–58. *Highe* (also *heighe*) can mean both "very much, strongly" as well as "high up, aloft." Literally, this passage reads, "There was never yet a pure creature in this life . . . so *very much* ravished in contemplation . . ., that there is not forever a *high* and wonderful cloud of unknowing between him and God." The twice-used *highe* ("very much, high") highlights that no matter how "advanced" or "high" you become in practicing contemplation, the cloud of unknowing rises with you, never leaving you. It's a given. It's always part of the process. The *ravischid* ("ravished") is the language of love that mysticism always adopts for its own, pure use.

3. The author's use of "leisure" (*leiser*) here is ironic, focusing attention on this chapter's analysis of what we usually

mean when we say that we "work" and are "busy." He is pointing out how uncomfortable we are with sitting still and doing what looks like "nothing" when we pray. We'd much rather look "busy," but, he insists, Mary *was* busy: *And therfore scheo had no* leiser *to listen to hir* ("And therefore she [Mary] had no *leisure time* to listen to her [Martha]"). See Gallacher, *The Cloud of Unknowing*, 49, line 866.

Chapter 18

1. The author's point is that some people see contemplation as "a waste of time," as *noght* ("nought, nothing") here. The concept of "nothing" is a central theme in the *Cloud*. See Gallacher, *The Cloud of Unknowing*, 50, line 884.

Chapter 20

1. The biblical passage discussed in this chapter is found in Luke 10:38–42: "Now as they went on their way, Jesus entered a certain village, where a woman named Martha welcomed him into her home. She had a sister named Mary, who sat at the Lord's feet and listened to what he was saying. But Martha was distracted by her many tasks; so she came to him and asked, 'Lord, do you not care that my sister has left me to do all the work by myself? Tell her then to help me.' But the Lord answered her, 'Martha, Martha, you are worried and distracted by many things; there is need of only one thing. Mary has chosen the best part, which will not be taken away from her.'"

2. The Middle English author has written something far more eloquent and to the point here than "You are wor-

ried": *Thou arte ful besy,* or "You are too busy," which should perhaps be the motto (or *mea culpa*) for our present age. It is certainly a leading reason for our persistent, profound worry. See Gallacher, *The Cloud of Unknowing*, 51, lines 938–39.

3. This "neighbors" is literally *even-Cristen* (or "fellow Christians"). But *even-Cristen* can also mean "neighbors," a word that sounds more inclusive and loving, so it was chosen here over the literal phrase. See Gallacher, *The Cloud of Unknowing*, 51, line 942.

4. "Good works" here is literally *besines was good.* This *besines* also means "activity" and "attention." In other words, Martha's "good" works, activities, or attention to worthy causes, also drew her "attention" away from God. See Gallacher, *The Cloud of Unknowing*, 51, line 943.

Chapter 21

1. This "hangs" is *hangeth.* See Gallacher, *The Cloud of Unknowing*, 53, line 979. The author has once again chosen diction conveying multiple concepts. Because *hangeth* can also mean "is suspended," this verb creates the image of a floating cloud and because it can mean "to be dependent on," *hangeth* connects the existence of this third stage with this cloud (and not with anything we do). Paradoxically, the physicality of the verb, *hangeth,* intensifies our understanding of the mystical nature of this last stage. We are at the end of words and at the beginning of spirit. And of course, as usual, the verb *hangeth* is a reminder of God's grace, that let his son "hang" on the Cross.

2. "Bother" is *medel* in Middle English ("meddle, interfere").

Literally, the writer is saying, "Don't meddle with contemplatives." *Medel yow not* is always good advice. See Gallacher, *The Cloud of Unknowing*, 53, line 998.

3. Here the Middle English noun *pley* ("play") has been translated into the contemporary verb, play. On the one hand, *pley* can be ironic, hinting at the taunt a contemplative might get—"You're not working; you're just playing." Literally, too, it implies that contemplative prayer is the work that is also the serious "play" of true (grown-up) "children" of God. See Gallacher, *The Cloud of Unknowing*, 53, line 999.

Chapter 22

1. John 20:11–15; Matthew 28:5–7.

2. This "studies" is *wil loke verrely in* ("will truly look at"). See Gallacher, *The Cloud of Unknowing*, 54, line 1014. The phrase could also have been translated, "Surely anyone who *really looks into* this Gospel story." The text up to this point has emphasized Mary's "looking." Literally, she cannot take her eyes off Jesus as Martha busies herself in the kitchen, and when Jesus died, Mary could not stop herself from looking for him, despite reassurances from angels that he had risen. This *loke* ("looks" or "studies") implies that just as Mary "looked" for Jesus, today we should look for him by studying the Gospels.

3. Throughout this chapter, the author has presented the traditionally accepted composite Mary: the unidentified sinner with the alabaster jar of ointment in Luke 7:37; Mary Magdalene in Luke 8:2; and Mary of Bethany in John 11:1–2. See Luke 7:40–50: "Jesus spoke up and said to him, 'Simon, I have something to say to you.'

'Teacher,' he replied, 'speak.' 'A certain creditor had two debtors; one owed five hundred denarii, and the other fifty. When they could not pay, he cancelled the debts for both of them. Now which of them will love him more?' Simon answered, 'I suppose the one for whom he cancelled the greater debt.' And Jesus said to him, 'You have judged rightly.' Then turning toward the woman, he said to Simon, 'Do you see this woman? I entered your house; you gave me no water for my feet, but she has bathed my feet with her tears and dried them with her hair. You gave me no kiss, but from the time I came in she has not stopped kissing my feet. You did not anoint my head with oil, but she has anointed my feet with ointment. Therefore, I tell you, her sins, which were many, have been forgiven; hence she has shown great love. But the one to whom little is forgiven, loves little.' Then he said to her, 'Your sins are forgiven.' But those who were at the table with him began to say among themselves, 'Who is this who even forgives sins?' And he said to the woman, 'Your faith has saved you; go in peace.'"

Chapter 23

1. This axiom, "God sends the cow, but not by the horn," is the Middle English version of "God helps those who help themselves." In the original, it reads: *God sendeth the kow, bot not by the horne.* See Gallacher, *The Cloud of Unknowing,* 55, line 1040.

Chapter 24

1. In Middle English, this sentence reads, *And as it is seyde of meeknes, how that it is sotely and parfitely comprehendid in this*

lityl blynde love put, *when it is betyng upon this derke cloude of unknowyng, alle other thinges* put *down and forgeten.*" See Gallacher, *The Cloud of Unknowing*, 55, lines 1057–59. The author makes a pun with the Middle English *put,* which can be both a noun meaning "a gentle blow," which I translated, "love tap" (as seen in the first instance in the quotation above), and a verb, *putten,* for "to push, to thrust," which I translated as "patted" (in the second instance above). In an effort to suggest this wordplay, I chose "tap" here for the noun (in "love tap") and "pat" as the verb (in "patted down"). The paronomasia in the original and its rhetorical emphasis are hard to duplicate.

Chapter 25

1. See 1 Corinthians 12:12–20.

Chapter 26

1. This "helped" (*holpin*) is from the Middle English verb, *holpen* ("to help"). See Gallacher, *The Cloud of Unknowing*, 58, line 1144. Today *holp* is still heard in Appalachia and elsewhere, though it's fast disappearing.

Chapter 28

1. American writer Ralph Waldo Emerson said, "Things are in the saddle and they ride mankind."

Chapter 31

1. The original diction here suggests the sort of "sleight of hand" maneuvering a magician needs to work feats of legerdemain: *Thou mayst seek sleightes and wiles and privé sotiltees of goostly sleightes to put hem [those thoughts]*

awey. See Gallacher, *The Cloud of Unknowing*, 60, lines 1212–13. Literally, this is "You may seek sleights and wiles and secret stratagems of spiritual subtlety to put those thoughts away."

Chapter 32

1. "God chose what is low and despised in the world, things that are not, to reduce to nothing things that are" (1 Corinthians 1:28).

Chapter 35

1. The book referred to here could be Walter Hilton's *Scale of Perfection,* for Hilton explains in chapter 15, *Thre meenys there ben whiche men most comonli use that yyven hem to contemplacioun: redynge of holi writ and of hooli techynge, goosteli meditacion, and besi praeris with devocioun.* ("There are three methods most commonly used to achieve contemplation: reading the divine word and its commentary, spiritual meditation, and diligent prayers with devotion.") See also chapters 23–24 of Hilton's *Scale of Perfection*. The book referred to could also be Guigo II's *Ladder,* the first three rungs of which are reading, reflecting, and praying, followed by a fourth rung, contemplation. In Middle English, these three exercises or "rungs" are *Lesson, Meditacion,* and *Oryson,* from the Latin, *lectio, meditation,* and *oratio.* The *lectio divina* (or "lesson" and "reading" here), step one, is a discipline far more profoundly engaged with a text than even the most attentive "reading." Lay or monastic, those practicing *lectio divina* steep themselves in the words of a text, becoming one with them, lingering over them, taking them into

the heart and mind deeply, repeatedly, slowly, meditatively, even memorizing the words. These three steps also correspond with the contemplative stages outlined by Origen, Denis the Areopagite, and other early mystic writers. These stages are purgation, illumination, and union.

2. The mirror is a traditional image for spiritual growth. Marguerite Porete (c. 1260–1310) writes: "If you want to understand what's in my book, *The Mirror of Simple Souls,* be careful what you say about it because it's very hard to comprehend. First, you must be overwhelmed by Humility. She's the keeper of Wisdom's coffers and the mother of every other virtue. Even you brilliant theologians and you smart students won't have any intellect for the *Mirror*—no matter if you're geniuses—if you don't read my book humbly. Only then can Love and Faith, the ladies of the house, help you rise above Reason." And Catherine of Siena (1347–1380) says in her *Dialogue:* "Make me a mirror of a good and holy life. Help me stay awake. Don't ever let me turn again to that miserable life I once lead in the darkness, through no fault of Your own. I didn't know Your truth then, so I didn't love it. But I do now" (Butcher, *A Little Daily Wisdom,* 12, 59).

Chapter 36

1. This "fully at ease, unruffled and restful," is *in a ful sad restfulness* in Middle English. See Gallacher, *The Cloud of Unknowing,* 65, lines 1357–58. The *sad* deserves special attention. It's from Old English and literally means "sated, satiated, surfeited; satisfied." In Middle English,

sad can also mean "firm, sure, steadfast, grave, sober, serious, dignified, solemn, discreet, wise, and pensive," as well as the expected "unhappy" and "sorrowful." The *sad* in the original text suggests that you can be so "satiated" with an awareness of your own sinfulness that it "sobers" your mind, making you "steadfast" and "wise."

Chapter 37

1. A reference to Matthew 6:7: "When you are praying, do not heap up empty phrases as the Gentiles do; for they think that they will be heard because of their many words." Benedict of Nursia also recommends in chapter 20 of his *Rule* that communal prayer must not be long-winded and pompous, but "brief and sincere."

Chapter 38

1. See Ephesians 3:18–19: "I pray that you may have the power to comprehend, with all the saints, what is the breadth and length and height and depth, and to know the love of Christ that surpasses knowledge, so that you may be filled with all the fullness of God."

Chapter 40

1. See the list of the seven deadly sins in chapter 10.

Chapter 44

1. See 2 Corinthians 7:9–11: "Now I rejoice, not because you were grieved, but because your grief led to repentance; for you felt a godly grief, so that you were not harmed in any way by us. For godly grief produces a repentance that leads to salvation and brings no regret,

but worldly grief produces death. For see what earnestness this godly grief has produced in you, what eagerness to clear yourselves, what indignation, what alarm, what longing, what zeal, what punishment! At every point you have proved yourselves guiltless in the matter."

2. In Middle English, this "exhausted and immersed in sorrow" is another memorable alliterative phrase: *al forsobbid and forsonken in sorow* ("entirely exhausted with sobbing and totally sunk in sorrow"). See Gallacher, *The Cloud of Unknowing*, 71, line 1552.

3. The "mount of perfection" alludes to Jesus's Sermon on the Mount; see Matthew 5:1–11.

4. In Middle English, this "But nowhere in this sorrow should you ever wish to not-be" is *And yit in al this sorrow he desireth not to unbe, for that were develles woodnes and despite unto God.* (Literally, "And yet in all this sorrow, he never desires to not-be, for that would be the madness of the devil and contempt of God.") See Gallacher, *The Cloud of Unknowing*, 72, lines 1573–74. The verb here is the Middle English infinitive *unben,* "to un-be" or "to cease to be." This peculiar negative construction shows that suicide is a willful "undoing" of something "done" by God. We can imagine Hamlet's saying in his famous speech, "To be or to un-be, that is the question."

Chapter 46

1. The Middle English reads here: *For sekirly what beestly herte that presumith for to touche the highe mounte of this werke, it schal be betyn awey with stones* ("For surely the beastly heart that presumes to touch the high mount of this [contemplative] work shall be beaten away with

stones"), presumably because the sinful "beastly heart" is daring to touch holiness. See Gallacher, *The Cloud of Unknowing*, 73, lines 1624–26. Compare Exodus 3:1–6: "Moses was keeping the flock of his father-in-law Jethro, the priest of Midian; he led his flock beyond the wilderness, and came to Horeb, the mountain of God. There the angel of the Lord appeared to him in a flame of fire out of a bush; he looked, and the bush was blazing, yet it was not consumed. Then Moses said, 'I must turn aside and look at this great sight, and see why the bush is not burned up.' When the LORD saw that he had turned aside to see, God called to him out of the bush, 'Moses, Moses!' And he said, 'Here I am.' Then he said, 'Come no closer! Remove the sandals from your feet, for the place on which you are standing is holy ground.' He said further, 'I am the God of your father, the God of Abraham, the God of Isaac, and the God of Jacob.' And Moses hid his face, for he was afraid to look at God."

2. In Middle English, this "foolish" is *sely,* the predecessor of our "silly." At the time that the *Cloud* manuscript was written, *sely* meant "innocent, harmless; foolish, gullible; doting; ignorant; weak, helpless, defenseless, hapless." See Gallacher, *The Cloud of Unknowing*, 73, line 1629.

3. In this chapter and the next, chapter 47, the diction and description suggest a game of hide-and-seek between parent and child, which ends with the parent "finding" the child and covering him or her with kisses and hugs. This image and ones similar to it are not unusual in devotional literature. In the thirteenth-century spiritual guidebook, *Ancrene Riwle,* another anonymous author writes, *Ure Louerd plaieth mid us, ase the moder mid hire*

junge deorlinge. ("Our Lord plays with us as the mother with her young darling.") The *Ancrene Riwle* passage then describes a hide-and-seek game in which God our Mother hides, her child cries out, "Mother! Mother!" and God jumps out with open arms and *cluppeth and cusseth and wipeth* ("hugs and kisses and wipes") our eyes. The *Ancrene Riwle* author uses this image to describe the experience of how God withdraws or "hides" his grace from us for a time, before returning to "find" us. For this passage, see Nicholas Watson, *Anchoritic Spirituality* (Mahwah, N.J.: Paulist Press, 1991), 132.

Chapter 47

1. In Middle English, this "led" is *sterid,* literally "steered," which is very close in sound to the verb *stired,* meaning "stirred," and the writer uses this resemblance to make a point. He was "led" by being "stirred" by God. See Gallacher, *The Cloud of Unknowing,* 74, line 1642.
2. "Cast" here is *castedest,* from *casten,* which can mean many things: "get rid of; throw in wrestling; defeat; hurl missiles at in war; cast a fishing net or lure," all of which seem to apply here.

Chapter 48

1. The *Cloud* author may be referring to Walter Hilton's *Scale of Perfection* again. See Clark and Dorward, *Walter Hilton: The Scale of Perfection,* 120 (book 1, 47).

Chapter 52

1. This translation is close to the original. The Middle English, *thei turne here brayne in here hedes* ("they turn their

brains in their heads"), is possibly the idiomatic origin for our contemporary phrase, "flip out," signifying a psychological inversion also known today as "going off the deep end." See Gallacher, *The Cloud of Unknowing*, 79, line 1814.

Chapter 53

1. *Sturdy scheep* were "afflicted with the brain disease sturdy" and acted "giddy, harebrained, wild." See Gallacher, *The Cloud of Unknowing*, 80, line 1832. This disease, also called "gid," affects herbivores, especially sheep, and is caused by the presence of tapeworm larvae in the brain, creating a fluid sac and making the sheep stagger. Sturdy sheep wheel around in circles. An early 1800s eyewitness account of this disease reports, "The symptoms of . . . [sturdy] . . . did not become aggravated till February, when the poor creature wandered from the rest of the flock, stood up against the fence, or fell into ditches." See William Dick, "On the Cure of Hydatids, or Sturdy, in Sheep, by Trepanning," *The Quarterly Journal in Agriculture*, 2 (Nov. 1829–Feb. 1831). The *Cloud* author writes here: *Som sette theire ighen in theire hedes as thei were sturdy scheep betyn in the heed, and as their schulde dighe anone.* ("Some [pseudo-contemplatives] fix their eyes in their heads, as if they were sturdy sheep beaten in the head, and as if they should die soon.") Perhaps the *betyn* means the sheep have been trepanned, to prolong life; or perhaps it means that they have been truly knocked ("beaten") in the head, to hasten their deaths. Either way, the image is not a pleasant one.

2. This remarkable passage is worth reading in the original: *Som ben evermore smyling and leighing at iche other worde that thei speke, as thei weren gigelotes and nice japyng jogelers lackyng kontenaunce.* If translated literally, it would read, "Some are always smiling and laughing at every other word that they speak, as if they were prostitutes and foolish, jesting clowns lacking all good manners." See Gallacher, *The Cloud of Unknowing*, 81, lines 1860–62. *Gigelotes* is our contemporary *gigolo*. This passage describes those people so addicted to getting attention that community means nothing to them.

Chapter 55

1. Literally, *prelates* ("prelates"), but "church leaders" is more ecumenical. See Gallacher, *The Cloud of Unknowing*, 82, line 1917.

2. The Middle English reads, *right as thei had cure of theire soules* ("as if they had [a responsibility for] the cure of their souls"). See Gallacher, *The Cloud of Unknowing*, 82–83, lines 1918–19. This responsibility is a heavy one and is not to be taken lightly nor approached without wise nuances. Gregory the Great provides us with an ancient but thoroughly up-to-date handbook on this topic—his sixth-century-A.D. *Liber Regulae Pastoralis*, or *Book of Pastoral Rule* (more commonly known as his *Pastoral Care*). The use of the Middle English *cure* here reminds me of the opening line of Gregory's book: *Pastoralis curae me pondera fugere*, where Gregory admits that an awareness of the burdens of pastoral care at first made him want to flee them. He then explains that pastors (and teachers)

must know their audience and be sensitive to the needs of the individuals to whom they minister.

3. The devil with one nostril is a common medieval image. This nostril is "fat and wide" (*grete and wyde*), reminding us that medieval physiognomy equates large noses with greed, lust, and heresy. See Gallacher, *The Cloud of Unknowing*, 83, line 1937. Demonic faces featuring only one nostril are also found in folkloric descriptions of vampires, banshees, some fairies, and giant ogres. Two nostrils were good. The thirteenth-century Victorine Thomas Gallus of Vercelli refers in his commentary on Isaiah 6 to their spiritual significance, saying that one nostril represents the intellect and the other represents *synderesis,* that spark of conscience motivating us to do good. See James Walsh, *The Pursuit of Wisdom and Other Works by the Author of "The Cloud of Unknowing"* (New York: Paulist Press, 1988), 66.

Chapter 56

1. "They and their friends place too much trust in their own opinions" is in the Middle English, *Thees . . . lenyn overmoche to theire owne knowyng* ("These . . . lean overmuch on their own understanding"), an allusion to Proverbs 3:5: "Trust in the LORD with all your heart and do not rely on your own insight." See Gallacher, *The Cloud of Unknowing*, 84, line 1959.

2. See Matthew 7:13–14: "Enter through the narrow gate; for the gate is wide and the road is easy that leads to destruction, and there are many who take it. For the gate is narrow and the road is hard that leads to life, and there are few who find it."

Chapter 57

1. This "looking" is unwise because it comes from a greedy desire to overreach natural boundaries. "Overreaching" is the etymological background of the word, *evil,* which originates in the Pre–Indo-European *upelo,* giving our word, *evil,* an original sense of "uppity, overreaching bounds." To understand the geography of this passage, we must also remember that medieval cosmology had unique features—the earth was a flat sphere on the ocean, the firmament was a thin metal half-cylinder above, and above that more water was found, with God living above these.

Chapter 58

1. See Matthew 25:31–46: "And the king will answer them, 'Truly I tell you, just as you did it to one of the least of these who are members of my family, you did it to me'" (40).

Chapter 59

1. See 1 Corinthians 15:44–53: "It is sown a physical body, it is raised a spiritual body. If there is a physical body, there is also a spiritual body. Thus it is written, 'The first man, Adam, became a living being'; the last Adam became a life-giving spirit. But it is not the spiritual that is first, but the physical, and then the spiritual. The first man was from the earth, a man of dust; the second man is from heaven. As was the man of dust, so are those who are of the dust; and as is the man of heaven, so are those who are of heaven. Just as we have borne the image of the man of dust, we will also bear the image of the

man of heaven. What I am saying, brothers and sisters, is this: flesh and blood cannot inherit the kingdom of God, nor does the perishable inherit the imperishable. Listen, I will tell you a mystery! We will not all die, but we will all be changed, in a moment, in the twinkling of an eye, at the last trumpet. For the trumpet will sound, and the dead will be raised imperishable, and we will be changed. For this perishable body must put on imperishability, and this mortal body must put on immortality."

2. The author is referring to Scholastic theologians, who taught that the new imperishable body would have this kind of agility.

3. John 3:13, 16. Also see Acts 1:6–11, for the Gospel story of the ascension of Jesus.

Chapter 60

1. For verses on the promise and gift of the Holy Spirit, see Acts 1:4–5, John 14:15–31, John 15:26, and Acts 2. And see James 1:17: "Every generous act of giving, with every perfect gift, is from above, coming down from the Father of lights, with whom there is no variation or shadow due to change."

2. See Philippians 3:20: "But our citizenship is in heaven, and it is from there that we are expecting a Savior, the Lord Jesus Christ."

3. See Matthew 6:21: "For where your treasure is, there your heart will be also."

Chapter 67

1. See John 10:34: "Jesus answered, 'Is it not written in your law, "I said, you are gods"?'" and Psalms 82:6: "I

say, 'You are gods, children of the Most High, all of you.'"

Chapter 69

1. This is a good example of the anonymous author's splendid ability to make prose poetic: *Wonderfuly is a mans affeccion varied in goostly felyng of this nought when it is noughwhere wrought.* See Gallacher, *The Cloud of Unknowing*, 95, lines 2318–19.

2. The author often uses *travayle* to indicate "the agony [of spiritual *labor*]." This word can also mean "the pains of childbirth"; therefore, it is a good choice to indicate "the pangs of spiritual rebirth." See Gallacher, *The Cloud of Unknowing*, 95, line 2323.

3. In *The Cloud of Unknowing*, Gallacher defines the Middle English word *stathil* ("root") as "the remaining root of a felled tree" (95), and in *The Cloud of Unknowing* and *The Book of Privy Counselling*, Hodgson defines it as "the remaining root" (228). This "felled tree" is rich with biblical allusion. Consider the tree of the knowledge of good and evil (Genesis 2:16–17) and Adam and Eve's "fall" when they ate of this tree. This image contrasts with Christ on the "tree" of the cross, when he "felled" or defeated the consequences of original sin. See Gallacher, *The Cloud of Unknowing*, 95, line 2337.

Chapter 70

1. See Matthew 13:8–9, quoting Jesus: "Other seeds fell on good soil and brought forth grain, some a hundredfold, some sixty, some thirty. Let anyone with ears listen!"

Chapter 71

1. This "awe-inspiring" is *feerdful* in Middle English and means what the original *awesome* does—"having the fear of God, reverent." It is a "good" terrifying, coming from a respect for God. See Gallacher, *The Cloud of Unknowing*, 97, line 2381.

2. See Exodus 24:15–18: "Then Moses went up on the mountain, and the cloud covered the mountain. The glory of the Lord settled on Mount Sinai, and the cloud covered it for six days; on the seventh day he called to Moses out of the cloud. Now the appearance of the glory of the Lord was like a devouring fire on the top of the mountain in the sight of the people of Israel. Moses entered the cloud, and went up on the mountain. Moses was on the mountain for forty days and forty nights." For Aaron, see Exodus 28 and Leviticus 8.

3. See 1 Corinthians 3:16: "Do you not know that you are God's temple and that God's Spirit dwells in you?"

4. See Exodus 24 and following notes.

Chapter 72

1. See Exodus 33:7–11a: "Now Moses used to take the tent and pitch it outside the camp, far off from the camp; he called it the tent of meeting. And everyone who sought the Lord would go out to the tent of meeting, which was outside the camp. Whenever Moses went out to the tent, all the people would rise and stand, each of them, at the entrance of their tents and watch Moses until he had gone into the tent. When Moses entered the tent, the pillar of cloud would descend and stand at the entrance of the tent, and the Lord would speak

with Moses. When all the people saw the pillar of cloud standing at the entrance of the tent, all the people would rise and bow down, all of them, at the entrance of their tents. Thus the Lord used to speak to Moses face to face, as one speaks to a friend."

Chapter 73

1. Exodus 25–27.

2. See Exodus 36:1–2: "Bezalel and Oholiab and everyone skillful to whom the Lord has given skill and understanding to know how to do any work in the construction of the sanctuary shall work in accordance with all that the Lord has commanded. Moses then called Bezalel and Oholiab and everyone skillful to whom the Lord had given skill, everyone whose heart was stirred to come to do the work."

3. This "helped" is another example of the Middle English verb *holpyn,* fossilized in the speech of some living in remote Appalachian towns to this day, as in "I'll be glad to holp you." See Gallacher, *The Cloud of Unknowing*, 98, line 2438.

4. "As simple as a child's" is *childly,* Middle English for "in the manner of a child or immature person; simply," with connotations of "foolish." See Gallacher, *The Cloud of Unknowing*, 99, line 2444. This carefully selected, self-deprecating word also alludes to Matthew 18:3, where Jesus is quoted as saying, "Truly I tell you, unless you change and become like *children,* you will never enter the kingdom of heaven," and also to 1 Corinthians 1:25: "For God's *foolishness* is wiser than human wisdom, and God's weakness is stronger than human strength [my emphasis]."

5. This "awkward" is *lewdely,* meaning "in an unlearned or ignorant fashion; ignorantly; unreasonably; also, unskillfully, incompetently, confusedly; in a simple or unsophisticated manner, simply; stupidly, foolishly, improvidently, carelessly." This apology is classic ancient rhetoric, and our anonymous author makes it repeatedly throughout his work. See Gallacher, *The Cloud of Unknowing,* 99, line 2444.

Chapter 74

1. This "easy" is *light,* an adjective also meaning "not heavy" or "less of a burden." However, as a noun, *light* means "illumination," which also fits the context. Our author is fully conscious of this semantic multiplicity when he chooses his diction. See Gallacher, *The Cloud of Unknowing,* 99, line 2459.
2. This "brown-nosers" is *gloser* in Middle English. *Gloser* comes from the verb *glosen,* meaning "to gloss (a text, a word), comment on, interpret, explain, paraphrase; to interpret (a text) falsely; to obscure the truth of (a matter), falsify (a statement)." By extension, a *gloser* is someone who "glosses" over the truth; in other words, a charming sycophant or flatterer. See Gallacher, *The Cloud of Unknowing,* 100, line 2477.

Chapter 75

1. Compare the message of Julian of Norwich (1342–1420), who wrote: "One day God spoke to me and I heard these words, 'You won't be overcome.' God wants us to pay attention to his words. God wants us

to be strong in our certainty in him, always, both in good times and in bad. The Lord loves us, and God so enjoys our company. God loves being with us and wants us to love him and enjoy being with him and trust him completely, and all will be well" (Butcher, *A Little Daily Wisdom,* 161).

2. "Best friend" is *ful freende,* literally, "full [or] complete friend." See Gallacher, *The Cloud of Unknowing,* 100, line 2506.

3. This "wise" is *hole* in Middle English and found in our modern words "hale, whole, health." See Gallacher, *The Cloud of Unknowing,* 101, line 2528. *Hole* goes back to Anglo-Saxon days, when its infinitive form, *gehælen,* meant "to heal, to save." The Old English word for "Savior" is *Hælend,* literally meaning, "the one who heals us and makes us whole." *Hælend* comes from the same root as *gehælen.* Also, this root is found in the Old English "Hello": *Wes þu hal,* literally, "May you be whole / hale / well." So when the *Cloud* author concludes this book by praying that his student may always experience "wise [*hole*] advice," the phrase literally means "advice that will *heal* you and make you *whole.*"

SUGGESTIONS FOR
FURTHER READING

Critical Editions and Selected Translations

Gallacher, Patrick J. *The Cloud of Unknowing*. TEAMS Middle English Text Series. Kalamazoo, Mich.: Western Michigan University Medieval Institute Publications, 1997, www.lib.rochester.edu/camelot/teams/cloud.htm.

Hodgson, Phyllis, ed. *The Cloud of Unknowing* and *The Book of Privy Counselling*. Early English Text Society Original Series Number 218. London: Humphrey Milford, 1944.

———. *The Cloud of Unknowing and Related Treatises (Analecta Cartusiana)*. Lewiston, N.Y.: Edwin Mellen Press, Ltd., 1999.

Johnston, William. *The Cloud of Unknowing and the Book of Privy Counseling*. New York: Doubleday, 2005. See page 7 for the quotation on the epigraph page.

McCann, Dom Justin, ed. *The Cloud of Unknowing and Other Treatises*. Westminster, Md.: The Newman Press, 1952.

Underhill, Evelyn. *The Cloud of Unknowing*. New York: Cosimo Classics, 2007.

Walsh, James, S.J. *The Cloud of Unknowing*. The Classics of Western Spirituality. Ramsey, N.J.: Paulist Press, 1981.

———. *The Pursuit of Wisdom and Other Works by the Author of "The Cloud of Unknowing."* New York: Paulist Press, 1988.

Wolters, Clifton. *The Cloud of Unknowing*. London: Penguin Books, 1978. See page 36 for the quotation on the epigraph page.

English Mysticism

Allen, Rosamund S. *Richard Rolle: The English Writings*. New York: Paulist Press, 1988. For a Middle English edition, see the *English Writings of Richard Rolle,* edited by Hope Emily Allen in 1931 for Oxford University Press.

Clark, John P. H., and Rosemary Dorward, trans. *Walter Hilton: The Scale of Perfection*. New York: Paulist Press, 1990.

Coleman, T. W. *English Mystics of the Fourteenth Century*. Whitefish, Mont.: Kessinger, 2004.

Colledge, Edmund, O.S.A., and James Walsh, S.J., trans. *Julian of Norwich Showings*. New York: Paulist Press, 1978.

Hodgson, Phyllis. *Three Fourteenth Century English Mystics*. London: Longmans, Green & Co., 1967.

Johnston, William, and Thomas Merton. *The Mysticism of the Cloud of Unknowing*. 2nd ed. New York: Fordham University Press, 2000.

Knowles, David. *The English Mystical Tradition*. London: Burns & Oates, 1961.

Morton, James. *The Ancrene Riwle: A Treatise on the Rules and Duties of Monastic Life*. London: Camden Society, 1853.

Tolkien, J. R. R., and N. P. Ker. *The English Text of the Ancrene Riwle: Ancrene Wisse, Corpus Christi College Cambridge MS 402*. Early English Text Society Original Series. London: Oxford University Press, 1997.

Watson, Nicholas. *Anchoritic Spirituality: Ancrene Wisse and Associated Works*. Mahwah, N.J.: Paulist Press, 1991.

Christian Mysticism

Chadwick, Henry. *St. Augustine Confessions.* Oxford: Oxford University Press, 1998.

Cohen, J. M., trans. *The Life of Saint Teresa of Avila by Herself.* New York: Penguin Classics, 1988.

Copp, John Dixon. *Dionysius the Pseudo-Areopagite: Man of Darkness / Man of Light.* New York: Edwin Mellen Press, Ltd., 2007.

Cousins, Ewert, trans. *Bonaventure: The Soul's Journey into God, the Tree of Life, the Life of St. Francis.* New York: Paulist Press, 1978.

Davis, Henry, trans. *St. Gregory the Great Pastoral Care.* New York: Newman Press, 1950.

Evans, G. R. *Bernard of Clairvaux.* New York: Harper Collins Spiritual Classics, 2005.

—————. *The Thought of Gregory the Great.* Cambridge: Cambridge University Press, 1986.

Gregg, Robert C., trans. *Athanasius: The Life of Antony and the Letter to Marcellinus.* New York: Paulist Press, 1980.

Hodgson, Phyllis, ed. *Deonise Hid Divinite and Other Treatises on Contemplative Prayer Related to "The Cloud of Unknowing."* London: Early English Text Society, 1955.

Kavanaugh, Kieran. *John of the Cross: Selected Writings.* New York: Paulist Press, 1987.

Martin, Dennis D. *Carthusian Spirituality: The Writings of Hugh of Balma and Guigo de Ponte.* New York: Paulist Press, 1997.

McEvoy, James J., ed. *Mystical Theology: The Glosses by Thomas Gallus and the Commentary of Robert Grosseteste De Mystica Theologia.* Dallas Medieval Texts and Translations 3. Oakville, Conn.: David Brown Book Company, 2003.

McGinn, Bernard. *The Essential Writings of Christian Mysticism.* New York: Modern Library, 2006.

———. *The Flowering of Mysticism: Men and Women in the New Mysticism—1200–1350. Presence of God: A History of Western Christian Mysticism,* vol. 3. New York: Herder & Herder, 1998.

———. *The Foundations of Mysticism: Origins to the Fifth Century. Presence of God: A History of Western Christian Mysticism,* vol. 1. New York: Herder & Herder, 1994.

———. *The Growth of Mysticism: Gregory the Great through the 12th Century. Presence of God: A History of Western Christian Mysticism,* vol. 2. New York: Herder & Herder, 1996.

McGinn, Bernard, and Patricia Ferris McGinn. *Early Christian Mystics: The Divine Vision of the Spiritual Masters.* New York: Crossroad Publishing Company, 2003.

Peers, E. Allison. *Dark Night of the Soul: A Masterpiece in the Literature of Mysticism by St. John of the Cross.* New York: Doubleday, 1959.

Rolt, C. E. *Dionysius the Areopagite: The Divine Names and the Mystical Theology.* Facsimile ed. Whitefish, Mont.: Kessinger, 1997.

Underhill, Evelyn. *Practical Mysticism: A Little Book for Normal People.* New York: Cosimo Classics, 2006.

Zinn, Grover A., trans. *Richard of St. Victor.* New York: Paulist Press, 1979.

Medieval Monasticism and Other Background Material

Barry, Patrick, O.S.B. *St. Benedict's Rule: A New Translation for Today.* Mahwah, N.J.: Hidden Spring, 2004.

Basu, Moni. "Zen Meets West, and Now, the South." *Atlanta*

Journal Constitution, August 3, 2007, A1, A10, www. buddhistchannel.tv/index.php?id=61,4596,0,0,1,0. See this article for the quotation on the epigraph page.

Butcher, Carmen Acevedo. *God of Mercy: Ælfric's Sermons and Theology.* Macon, Ga.: Mercer University Press, 2006.

————. *Hildegard of Bingen, Doctor of the Church: A Spiritual Reader:* Brewster, Mass.: Paraclete Press, 2013.

————. *Man of Blessing: A Life of St. Benedict.* Brewster, Mass.: Paraclete Press, 2012.

Dick, William. "On the Cure of Hydatids, or Sturdy, in Sheep, by Trepanning." *The Quarterly Journal in Agriculture* 2 (Nov. 1829–Feb. 1831).

Elliston, Michael. See Moni Basu entry.

Feiss, Hugh. *Essential Monastic Wisdom: Writings on the Contemplative Life.* San Francisco: HarperSanFrancisco, 2000.

Goleman, Daniel. *Destructive Emotions: A Scientific Dialogue with the Dalai Lama.* New York: Bantam, 2003.

Kelly, John. *The Great Mortality: An Intimate History of the Black Death, the Most Devastating Plague of All Time.* New York: HarperCollins, 2005.

King, Ursula. *Christian Mystics: Their Lives and Legacies throughout the Ages.* Mahwah, N.J.: HiddenSpring, 2001.

Lawrence, C. H. *Medieval Monasticism: Forms of Religious Life in Western Europe in the Middle Ages.* 3rd ed. New York: Longman, 2000.

Maguire, Nancy Klein. *An Infinity of Little Hours: Five Young Men and their Trial of Faith in the Western World's Most Austere Monastic Order.* New York: Public Affairs, 2006.

Massimo, Riva, and Michael Papio, eds. The Decameron Web, www.brown.edu/Departments/Italian_Studies/ dweb/dweb.shtml.

Meyendorff, John. *Byzantine Theology: Historical Trends and Doctrinal Themes.* 2nd ed. New York: Fordham University Press, 1987.

Pope, John C., ed. *Homilies of Ælfric: A Supplementary Collection.* 2 vols. EETS 259, 260. London: Oxford University Press, 1967–68.

Pullman, Bernard. *The Atom in the History of Human Thought.* Oxford: Oxford University Press, 2001.

Taylor, Cheryl. "Paradox upon Paradox: Using and Abusing Language in *The Cloud of Unknowing* and Related Texts." *Parergon* 22, no. 2 (July 2005).

Tixier, René. "'Þis louely blinde werk': Contemplation in *The Cloud of Unknowing* and Related Treatises." *In Mysticism and Spirituality in Medieval England,* edited by William F. Pollard and Robert Boenig. Woodbridge, Suffolk, U.K.: Boydell & Brewer, 1997.

Tuchman, Barbara. *The Distant Mirror: The Calamitous Fourteenth Century.* New York: Ballantine Books, 1996.

Ward, Benedicta. *Miracles and the Medieval Mind.* Philadelphia: University of Pennsylvania, 1987.

Ziegler, Philip. *The Black Death.* New York: HarperCollins, 1971.

Useful Reference Resources

Algeo, John, and Carmen Acevedo Butcher. *Origins and Development of the English Language.* 7th ed. Boston: Wadsworth Cengage Learning, 2014.

Algeo, John, and Carmen Acevedo Butcher. *Problems in the Origins and Development of the English Language.* 7th ed. Boston: Wadsworth Cengage Learning, 2014.

Kurath, Hans, and Sherman M. Kuhn, eds. *Middle English*

Dictionary. Ann Arbor, Mich.: University of Michigan Press, 1952–2001.

Lewis, Robert E., ed. *Middle English Dictionary. Plan and Bibliography*. 2nd ed. Ann Arbor, Mich.: University of Michigan Press, 2007.

McSparran, Frances, ed. *Middle English Dictionary*. http://quod.lib.umich.edu/m/med/.

Metzger, Bruce M., senior ed. *The New Revised Standard Version of the Bible. (Anglicized Edition)*. New York: The Division of Christian Education of the National Council of the Churches of Christ in the United States of America, 1995, www.devotions.net/bible/oobible.htm.

Migne, Jacques Paul. *Patrologiae Cursus Completus . . . Series Latina (Latin Patrology)*. Paris: Migne, 1844–55. 221 volumes.

SHAMBHALA POCKET LIBRARY

AFTER IKKYŪ
Jim Harrison

THE ART OF PEACE
Morihei Ueshiba

BECOME WHAT YOU ARE
Alan Watts

THE BODHISATTVA GUIDE
His Holiness the Fourteenth Dalai Lama

THE BOOK OF TEA
Kakuzo Okakura

THE CLOUD OF UNKNOWING
Translated by Carmen Acevedo Butcher

THE DHAMMAPADA
Translated and edited by Gil Fronsdal

I CHING
Translated by Thomas Cleary